Endorsem...

"I was deeply blessed by this book and Brenda's gentle wisdom. As mothers, it so often feels as though we just can't get it right. We are tired and overwhelmed, and while we have vision for our roles as mothers, some days it seems impossible to connect our vision with the dailyness of mothering. Brenda Jacobson is a mentor mom who graciously comes alongside us younger moms and helps us navigate this awesome and exhausting mothering world with personal examples, Scripture, and the wisdom of experience and faithful perseverance. *Something to Stand On* is rich, deep, and practical. It's sure to give life and peace to a mama's heart and real hope and help for the day-in and day-out of this wild ride called mothering."

~SARAH MAE, author of *Desperate:
Hope for the Mom Who Needs to Breathe*

"Where was *Something to Stand On* fifteen years ago? This book had me at "not so exhausting" in the subtitle! The last thing any mom needs is one more book telling her why she's not doing everything she's supposed to be doing; what EVERY mom needs is an experienced mentor who picks us up at our weariest and weakest point, dusts us off, and outlines how to live in freedom. Brenda Jacobson provides exactly that in this much-needed resource. With tough love and biblical wisdom, Brenda reminds moms that our families CAN and WILL flourish when we keep our own hearts focused on God. Brenda not only challenges readers to speak out loud to God but to wait expectantly, listen, and write what they experience. Brenda gets me, and she'll get you too!"

~SAMI CONE, bestselling author of *Raising Uncommon Kids*, blogger (*SamiCone.com*),
TV personality, and editor-in-chief of *Babywise.life & BabyEarth.com*)

"I've learned so many wonderful things about mothering by watching Brenda Jacobson over the years. I've always admired her wisdom, as well as her quiet but powerful style of parenting. Now she's sharing with all of us her wealth of experience and godly advice through her new book, *Something to Stand On*. Every mom is going to want to grab this one!"

~LISA JACOBSON,
Club31Women.com

"Though we have access to more information than any other generation of parents, babies still don't come with instruction books. Moms are overwhelmed at all they think they are supposed to do and often forget God is with them in the process, preparing them for this task. Brenda Jacobson's workbook *Something to Stand On* helps moms remember how they have been uniquely created to parent and hear directly from God. A practical tool that weaves Brenda's gentle voice in with places for the reader to reflect and apply to her own life, there is nothing quite like this available to moms. A great resource for churches, MOPS groups, and moms to do on their own with Brenda's online mentoring, as together we remember we have something to stand on."

~ALEXANDRA KUYKENDALL,
author and cofounder of *The Open Door Sisterhood*

"Brenda is the mom mentor we all wish we had. Even after raising one son to adulthood yet still having a four-year-old in the house, I need Brenda's wisdom! Whether you're a new mom or find yourself in a parenting slump, there is gold for you in this book. It will empower you to parent with boldness and confidence!"

~KATE MERRICK, author of *And Still She Laughs* and
Here, Now, homeschooling mom of three

"*Something to Stand On* is a breath of fresh air for mamas in all stages. Within the first few pages I was challenged, convicted, and deeply encouraged. I've never thought of parenthood like this before. I'm so thankful to Brenda for sharing her years of mothering wisdom with us in this book. I'm soaking in every word and know I will be returning to read it again and again."

~KAREN STOTT, founder of Pursuit Community
and author of *An Intentional Life: A Life-Giving Invitation
to Uncover Your Passions and Unlock Your Purpose*

"Most moms long for a seasoned voice they can follow and trust on the path of mothering, but it is rare to find. Brenda Jacobson fills that void with time-tested, wise, and bedrock truth. In this valuable workbook, she doesn't just offer us solid biblical guidance, she helps us transfer that knowledge into our real lives with our real families. Moms of this generation, this is a must-have book you didn't even know you needed!"

~KRISTA GILBERT, author of *Reclaiming Home:
A Family's Guide to Life, Love, and Legacy*,
and host of *The Open Door Sisterhood Podcast*

"How many times have I heard in my parenting journey to "walk by faith," or "to entrust my children to the Lord?" Such wonderful advice, and yet, as a new mom trying to simply survive the little years, there were times I wondered, '*How exactly do I do that?!*' I wish I had held this book in my hands back then! Brenda Jacobson's words breathe life into the harried heart of any mom who is asking the same question, no matter her stage of parenting. She teaches her how to create a firm foundation in the Lord. Drawing from her own experience as a mom and mentor, Brenda leads moms straight to the heart of God. With practical, applicable teaching and action steps, prompts for personal reflection, and truth from God's Word, moms can begin to change their motherhood journey to bring glory to God and healing to their homes from the moment they open these pages. The next generation will be blessed by mothers who have hidden their hearts in Christ, and who have taken these words to heart."

~KRISTEN KILL, **author of** *Finding Selah:*
The Simple Practice of Peace When You Need It Most

"I've known and respected Brenda for years. We've encouraged one another to trust God through the joys and challenges of raising children in this broken world. She's an honest and godly woman, and this is a book full of graceful wisdom for parents."

~JUDY UNDERWOOD,
cofounder of *RECENTERED GROUP*

something to stand on

BUILDING A FOUNDATION
FOR PARENTING THAT'S
PURPOSEFUL, EFFECTIVE,
& NOT SO EXHAUSTING

BRENDA JACOBSON
with MELISSA BINDER

ⓩ | ZEALbooks

Published by Zeal Books
PO Box 80945
Portland, OR 97280 USA
www.zealbooks.com

This is a work of nonfiction. The events and experiences detailed herein are all true and have been faithfully rendered. Some names and identities have been changed in order to protect the privacy of certain individuals involved.

Cover Design: Rachel Jacobson, Rachel Jacobson Studio
Interior Design: Katherine Lloyd, The Desk

Library of Congress Cataloging-in-Publication Data

Names: Jacobson, Brenda, author | Binder, Melissa, author
Title: Something to stand on: building a foundation for parenting that's purposeful, effective, & not so exhausting / Brenda Jacobson, Melissa Binder
Description: Portland: Zeal Books, 2018
Identifiers: LCCN 2018956775 | ISBN 97800999055762 (paperback)
ISBN 9780999055779 (ebook)
Subjects: LCSH: Family & Relationships—Parenting | Motherhood
Classification data is on file with the Library of Congress

Printed in the United States of America
First Edition 2018

18 19 20 21 22 23 24 BP 7 6 5 4 3 2 1

Dedication

To John Van Diest,

The world knows you as an entrepreneur, an author, and a publisher, but to me you are Dad. You modeled Christ to me all through my childhood, and you continue to model him today. You put your life on hold for ten years to selflessly take care of Mom. At eighty-six years old, you continue to drive your weekly Meals on Wheels route delivering food to the elderly, most of whom are younger than you. You are my hero.

Contents

PARENTING A NEW WAY (three weeks)

FINISHING WELL (one week)

Introduction

I tell you not to worry about everyday life. . . .
Can all your worries add a single moment to your life?

MATTHEW 6:25, 27

It was afternoon. A Thursday, maybe. And I was where I spent most afternoons: behind the wheel of our blue Suburban. My eyes were on the road, my mind on my to-do list. I had to taxi our four children to and from school, friends' houses, and basketball practices, and then cook dinner and oversee homework. Jerseys needed to be washed before Friday's game. I had to plan Bible study questions for my time with the church's high school girls the next day, and I'd forgotten—again—to email our small group with details for our potluck next week. I was way behind on organizing a fundraiser for the new local Christian school, but it—

I couldn't even finish the thought.

For right then and there, on a straight stretch of Highway 97, it hit me.

There I was, so concerned about being a good mother, yet I was spending precious moments with my children worrying about my schedule, completely emotionally removed from the four in the backseat. Worse, I had been emotionally removed from the Lord.

I rarely had time for God those days. I sprang out of bed, sprinted for seventeen hours, and collapsed into bed. I was pouring out, out, out and not making time to be filled up. I said I trusted him, but relinquishing any control of my life to God was out of the question. I couldn't risk dropping any of the balls I was juggling.

But that ordinary day, on the way home from picking up the kids from school, something changed.

I saw my life for what it was: impressive on the outside, but increasingly hollow at the core. In an effort to please the Lord, I had added one good thing after another to my to-do list until, without even noticing, I'd let time with the Lord disappear from my list altogether. Once the top priority, it had been pushed down by activities I thought would please him. I was great at doing—not so much at simply being. I felt like I was constantly running—trying to keep up, trying to stay balanced on shifting ground. I had nothing firm to stand on.

This wake-up call sparked a quest to reorder my life with God at the center—relationship with him as the foundation for everything else. The more time I gave to my relationship with the Lord, the more he filled me. The more changes I made to live life his way, the more wonderful life was. For the first time in years I felt truly content and full. I noticed that I had more energy, more patience, and more insight for all the little demands of each day. I had the wisdom to draw healthy boundaries in my schedule. I began to parent my children with long-term vision and purpose. That year, it dawned on me that the health of my own spiritual life was fundamental to my parenting. And as my life changed, my children's lives did as well. After all, they learned from watching me.

This workbook is for moms who are longing for something to be different. It's for women who are exhausted, scattered, and anxious. It's for women who feel aimless and long for purpose in their lives and their parenting. It's for women who want to be the best moms they can be for their kids. After raising my own four children to adulthood and mentoring dozens of moms—from ex-cons in the city to upper-middle-class gals in the suburbs—I know what works, and it's not a list of tips and tricks. A new philosophy is not something to stand on. The latest science is not something to stand on. But a foundation in the Lord is.

Each chapter in this workbook is a step in laying that foundation. These new perspectives will help you remove barriers between yourself and your King, opening up communication and connection so you can be filled—with energy, with wisdom, with purpose. Because you know what? Good parenting starts with you. If you want to see changes in your children, in your parenting, you must start with changes in your own heart. And you know what else? The Lord is waiting eagerly to be your foundation. He is in the business of healing hearts, families, and relationships, and he's inviting you in—right now—with your disappointment, your bad choices, and your fear.

In the middle of your chaotic life, he is waiting to provide peace. In the middle of the mundane, he is waiting with adventure. When you cry in the shower out of sheer exhaustion, he is waiting. When you snap at your child and instantly regret it, he is waiting. When your child reaches out to someone in kindness and you beam, he is waiting. He is waiting to celebrate your victories and forgive your mistakes. He is waiting to finally be the firm foundation beneath your feet. He is waiting for the same with your children.

I will be honest with you: building a foundation is hard work. You will be asked to examine your heart and your life in uncomfortable ways, and you will be pushed to take practical steps toward life God's way. But I believe you will also find it remarkably transforming. I believe you will discover greater purpose in your life and a clearer vision for your parenting. I believe you will be rejuvenated with unexpected energy, wisdom, and self-control. I believe you will see changes in your family that you never thought possible. I believe that, like me, you will stop running and have something strong to stand on.

How to Use This Workbook

1. **Ideally, find a mentor before you begin.** This workbook is designed to be completed in combination with a mentor relationship. You need another woman—preferably someone older and wiser—to walk through this journey with you. Your mentor will be able to help you process what you're learning, and she'll help you apply some of the practical assignments to your own unique situation. If you don't have someone in your life you can ask to be a mentor, ask a leader at your church to introduce you to someone. Your pastor or director of women's ministry can likely recommend a woman in your community, and you'll benefit from developing a positive new relationship. If finding a mentor isn't an option for you, please visit www.somethingtostandon.com for opportunities to engage in an online mentoring community.

2. **Take your time.** The chapters in this workbook are designed to be tackled one week at a time. You can move slower—some of these chapters are quite challenging—but don't move any faster. It's just too much.

3. **Pause if you need to.** There are several parts in this workbook where I recommend talking with a counselor if you face certain challenging situations or personal struggles. Close the workbook and at least begin dealing with those issues before you move forward. There's no reason to power through when you have something else in your life that needs to be addressed. You'll get more out of the workbook if you allow for this pause.

4. **Back of the book.** Pages have been created for your own Personal Journal when additional space is needed for writing down your thoughts.

LAYING THE GROUNDWORK

TWO WEEKS

In this section, we aim to establish a vision for godly parenting and encourage a thankful heart, which will enable us to experience the goodness of the Father and prepare our hearts for the hard work ahead.

1

foundational parenting

Direct your children onto the right path,
and when they are older, they will not leave it.

PROVERBS 22:6

I remember the nurse wheeling me to the curb outside the hospital the day after my oldest, Danae, was born. My husband, Don, placed our precious daughter into her car seat, trying to be as gentle as possible, acting like he knew what he was doing. On our drive home, a car blazed through a yellow light as we pulled to a stop. "That driver is so irresponsible!" Don barked. I smiled at his protectiveness, thinking that before Danae's birth he would have done the same thing and thought nothing of it. Everything had changed.

I anticipated that navigating this new life would be exciting and overwhelming. In my heart, I bravely vowed to become the very best mom I could be and raise my daughter to change the world for the Lord. I wanted to provide her with every opportunity. But these lofty ambitions soon gave way to changing poopy diapers, soothing a crying baby, feeding, folding mountains of laundry, changing more diapers, and more feeding. This sleep-deprived phase was a blur—the only distinction between day and night was my husband's location and the amount of light coming through the windows. I had gone from businesswoman to milk machine. When I finally got my feet on the ground and felt almost like my old self, it started all over again with baby number two.

Personal Reflection

What lofty dreams did you cling to when you first became a mother?

What dreams do you still hold for your children today?

As my children outgrew diapers and their personalities began to emerge, my Super Mom dreams resurfaced. I wanted my children to have godly characters, and I aspired to lovingly discipline and teach them God's path. I was consistent in my effort to correct bad behavior and sour attitudes. I followed through with consequences when the correction didn't stick.

But in the midst of busyness, my Survivor Mom habits often dominated and my motives blurred. I frequently corrected their tone or behavior because it annoyed me, made my life harder, or reflected poorly on me as a parent—not because I was focused on leading them toward God. I engaged with my children regularly, but typically stopped short of addressing the heart issues behind their behavior. I was regularly complimented for how well-behaved my children were, but in my gut, something felt wrong.

Today, I call this Behavioral Parenting. This approach focuses on proper behavior and discipline. Behavioral moms are focused on raising good kids—which is not the same thing as raising godly ones. This style often looks great to observers. But, in reality, Behavioral Parenting is selfish and fails to instill lasting character. It's also not uncommon for this style to result in a wedge between moms and their adult children.

Another common approach is Passive Parenting. Instead of constantly correcting or scolding their children, Passive moms are generally disengaged and hands-off. These are the moms with

> **PARENTING TIP**
>
> *If you catch yourself responding to misbehavior with anger, check your motives. Are you more concerned about shaping your child's heart or about how your child's behavior affects you?*

their eyes fixed ahead in the grocery store, ignoring their children as the little ones plead for attention or candy. The Passive mom's goal is generally to avoid conflict and conserve energy. When her child refuses to pick up his toys, a Passive mom might simply do it for him or leave the mess without following through on any consequence. She might hold a philosophical view that consequences limit or damage children, but more often she simply doesn't have the emotional energy to follow through. Like Behavioral Parenting, Passive Parenting is ultimately selfish and fails to empower children with the skills and character they need.

Personal Reflection

Overall, do you lean toward Behavioral Parenting or Passive Parenting? Give a couple recent examples.

Think back to the examples you just listed. Why did you respond the way you did? (For instance, maybe you were in the presence of someone whose opinion matters to you, afraid of causing a scene in public, trying to multitask, or simply exhausted.)

How did your responses affect your child's heart?

What I didn't see as a young mom was that my behavior-based approach to parenting flowed out of a much larger reality in my life at the time: behavior-based living.

Since I was a child, my heart's desire has been to please the Lord. As a young woman, I had a passion to raise my children well and to teach them to love the Lord. But as my life became a juggling act, I became rigid. My relationship with the Lord took a backseat while I attempted to keep up behavior I thought would please him. I was working hard to perform at a surface level, and I expected my family to fall in line as well.

Our approach to raising children is often a reflection of our approach to life. A Passive mom who avoids conflict with her child probably avoids conflict with her spouse, friends, family, and colleagues. She may work hard to keep her environment peaceful above all else—she just wants to feel comfortable, secure, or happy. She may want desperately to be liked by her children and believe that angering them will hurt her standing in their eyes.

In both cases, the root cause is the same: there is no firm foundation. Both Behavioral and Passive Parenting moms are genuinely trying to do their best, but they're doing so without something solid to stand on.

Personal Reflection

How does your tendency to fall into Behavioral Parenting or Passive Parenting reflect broader patterns in your life?

There is an alternative. I call it Foundational Parenting, and it only exists in the context of Foundational Living, a life built on the Rock. A Foundational life is one of thriving, not just surviving. It is a life rooted in your story and relationship with the Lord. It is a life of surrender— where God sits on the throne, not you.

Foundational Parenting is about cultivating a healthy heart, mind, and spirit in your child. That is, establishing a strong foundation—giving them something to stand on. It also requires a strong foundation in you. Moms living a Foundational Life know that their ultimate purpose in life is to glorify the Lord by pursuing relationship with him and becoming more and more like Christ. They are able to love, see, and nurture their children because they feel loved, seen, and nurtured by God. They are able to lead their children in addressing the root issues in their young hearts because they have already learned to deal with the root issues in their own.

Personal Action

In the space below, write a life purpose you can refer to as a reminder that, ultimately, your only purpose in life is to love and glorify the Lord. For example, here's how I wrote mine: "My purpose is to be fully dedicated to my Savior Jesus with all my heart, soul, and mind."

Ultimately, this workbook is about helping you lead a Foundational Life so you can be a Foundational Parent. Week by week, we'll build a strong foundation in the Lord—something you can stand on as you parent your children with purpose. Something you can pass on to them as they grow.

One of the first steps is addressing our own selfishness. You see, at the core of Foundational Parenting is true selflessness. A Foundational mom plays the long game. Because she is filled up by God, she can take time to engage with her child on a heart level, even if the day already feels too hectic to handle. She initiates hard conversations, choosing to endure uncomfortable tension for the sake of her child's developing character.

Although it's an essential first step, recognizing our own selfishness is tricky. We love our children deeply, and it's hard to see that our decisions might be more in service to our own needs than theirs. We're masters at justifying our actions, and it takes a massive perspective shift to see ourselves in a new light.

I recently walked with my friend Rhonda through this kind of reorientation. She is a loving single mom working a full-time job. Understandably, she's exhausted and stretched thin—and has been for years. Recently, she sent me this message:

Brenda, I could use some prayer. I feel like I'm failing as a mom. I am not being as consistent as I need to be. Katie is being really disrespectful at home, in school, and at church. Heidi is talking back and throwing a fit if I tell her "no." Katherine is always whining and doesn't want to do what's asked. I know a lot of it is my fault. I don't follow through with what I say and it's just a lot of talking I do. I yell a lot again. I don't want it to be this way and I know I'm the only one who can make it better. There is not enough space in our small apartment. I am feeling like I'm at work all the time and barely have time to do the things that need to be done, like parenting the right way. I feel like there is not enough time in the day to do everything that needs to be done and for the girls to get to bed at an appropriate time. Sorry for writing a book!

Rhonda shared with me later that, in the weeks leading up to our conversation, she'd spent a lot of time in the evenings on her phone. Her days at work were long and tiring, and she just wanted a mental break when she got home. We discussed the reality that her little girls didn't see it that way. They'd been apart from Rhonda all day, and they were desperate for her attention. They knew that as long as they behaved well, she remained disengaged. They discovered that when they misbehaved, she looked up from the screen and focused on them—even if it was just to yell. Katie, Heidi, and Katherine took what they could get. Besides, they'd learned their mom gave them second, third, and fourth chances before exacting discipline. Being yelled at wasn't ideal, but it was better than being ignored. So they continued to act out and she continued to yell, retreating deeper into her phone out of irritation.

Personal Reflection

Does this scenario remind you of any unhealthy patterns in your home life? Explain.

Rhonda wasn't handling her evenings well, and I think we can all agree it was causing problems for everyone in the home. But, at the same time, we can empathize with her. Who wouldn't need a mental break after a long day at work? Her family might have been in a rough patch, but we're slow to call her selfish. She was overwhelmed and tired and maybe not handling it superbly, but who could blame her?

Let me ask you this: How would your response change if I told you Rhonda was a nanny to Katie, Heidi, and Katherine? That the girls belonged to another family, and she was entrusted with caring for them? I suspect your feelings might change. You might even feel a little angry. In that scenario, Rhonda starts to look lazy and selfish. She has no right to treat the kids that way.

Take it one step further: imagine these girls were princesses in a monarchy. Now picture the king peeking into the room and seeing Rhonda, the family nanny, slumped on the couch, looking at her phone while the kids vied for her attention. Imagine the king saw Rhonda look up only to yell angrily at the princesses. Rhonda would likely be fired on the spot. After all, it's a huge privilege to be employed by the king. It's her job to raise these girls into young women fit to serve the kingdom, regardless of whether or not she's tired at the end of the day.

Personal Reflection

Imagine your children were actually princes and princesses in the British royal house, and that you were their guardian. Name three to five things you know you'd do differently.

Do you see where this is going?

Rhonda's children do not belong to her. Your children do not belong to you. They are the Lord's, and he has placed them in your home, that you might raise them to serve the kingdom well. Foundational Parenting isn't just about doing what's best for your children because you love them. It's about doing what's best for your children because they are the King's.

Does that mean we can't carve out time to rest and take care of ourselves? Of course not. We need breaks in order to be good nannies. Does that mean God will fire us if we mess up? Absolutely not. There is grace abundant for you, and children are very forgiving. Does it mean we all have some work to do? Yes. And that's exactly what this workbook is designed to help you do.

Personal Reflection

Reflect on the idea that you are a nanny or guardian to God's children. What thoughts and feelings does that stir in you? Know that it's OK to feel guilt or shame right now. Write a short prayer of confession to the Lord.

Name one way in which you've been selfish lately, and reflect on how you can forfeit that this week.

A good nanny is not good simply because she knows the right disciplinary tricks—she's good because she loves deeply, respects her boss, and responds to children with love, grace, justice, and consistency. Her character traits are even more important than her job skills. So are yours.

For the next thirteen weeks, we're going to remain focused on your own heart with the goal of guiding you into deeper self-awareness and relationship with the Lord. We'll explore our life stories, grow in obedience, and learn how to surrender our life to the Lord, allowing him to change our heart. It is only from this place of connection to your life-giving Savior that you and your family can flourish. In the final section of this workbook, we'll shift our focus more directly toward your kids and tackle the toughest aspects of parenting: allowing our children to experience pain, setting healthy boundaries, navigating discipline, and parenting with long-term purpose.

Personal Action

In the space below, write a one-sentence job description you can use throughout the day to remind yourself that you have been entrusted with God's children. As an example, here's a job description I wrote for myself: "I am a nanny for my children, lovingly preparing them for their King."

You have freedom to write a description that's right for you. If you don't like "nanny," choose another word that captures a similar idea, such as "caretaker," "guardian," or "coach." You're also welcome to craft your own version of what you're raising them to do or be. For instance, you might write a job description more like this: "I am a coach to Jack and Laura, lovingly training them to flourish in God's kingdom." The basic template is this: "I am a [nanny, coach, mentor, or other noun] to [children's names], lovingly [training, preparing, equipping, or other verb] them [to flourish in God's kingdom, for service to the King, to be life-long disciples of Jesus, or other description of vision]."

Now, copy your job description onto an index card. Put it somewhere you'll see it frequently, such as on the refrigerator or bathroom mirror.

Rocket Prayer

One of the main goals in this workbook is to lead you in cultivating a rich prayer life. Many women find prayer awkward and unrewarding. Some can't even fathom having enough time in their day to pray. Rocket prayers are a powerful, accessible practice for all women, no matter where they are in relation to prayer. These prayers don't even require a "dear God" or an "amen."

There are only two things to know. First, a rocket prayer is short. Even just three words, such as "give me insight," counts. Second, a rocket prayer is a request for God to change your own heart—not change your child, your husband, or the stranger who cut you off in the grocery line. "Help my husband calm down" or "make my child listen" do not count. Rocket prayers are about asking God to help you handle your end of the situation with wisdom, love, and kindness.

No matter how busy you are, you have time for these prayers. Train yourself to insert three-second pauses throughout your day to call on God for wisdom, insight, or a change of heart. Each week, I'll include a recommended rocket prayer. Here's this week's:

"Lord, help me remember these children belong to you."

Say this prayer when you go into your child's bedroom in the morning. Say this prayer when your child throws a fit over breakfast. Say this prayer when your child scores the winning goal. This little prayer helps us stay centered in Foundational Parenting, focusing our eyes on the King and prioritizing our child's needs over our own.

Prayer of Response

Before you close this workbook for the rest of the week, take a few minutes to write a prayer of response to God. First, thank him for ways he has been good to you. Then, tell him what you're thinking and feeling as you process what you've learned.

Pass It On

Consider inviting your children into what you've learned this week by creating an opportunity to pass on the essentials: that they are God's children and he's entrusted you with the job of raising them.

Try reading a book about a royal family at bedtime. When the book is over, ask your child if he knows he's a prince, too, and work your way to the message you want to hit home. For instance, your side of the conversation might look like this: "Carter, did you know you're a prince? Well you are. God is king of the whole world, and you are his son. And do you know what my job is? That's right—at work I am an accountant. But it's also my job to be your mom, and I love that job most. But because you are God's son, my job isn't just to raise you however I want. My job is to raise you the way God wants, because you are his prince. Now, I don't always do a good job, but I want you to know I'm trying to help you become a good prince."

If your child is old enough, you might even invite him to brainstorm with you about character traits a prince needs to learn. For instance, you might decide together that a good prince needs to be fair, generous, and smart. This can come in handy later. The next day, when that same boy is refusing to share a toy with his sister, you can say, "Hey Carter, do you remember how we decided that a good prince needs to learn to be generous? This is an opportunity for you to practice generosity."

2

living thankfully

Be thankful in all circumstances,
for this is God's will for you who belong to Christ Jesus.

1 THESSALONIANS 5:18

When my son Blair was fourteen, we went in for a routine physical before the start of basketball season. The doctor discovered a heart murmur and ordered an echocardiogram. Technicians stared at the screen, measured, and whispered to one another while I watched nervously. Finally, the doctor spoke with steady, practiced confidence: "Blair has a hole in his heart the size of a quarter and needs open-heart surgery. Without it, he might die."

He kept talking, but I stopped listening after the word "die."

We drove home in silence to a cold, dark house. Blair went to his room and shut the door. I fell onto the couch in utter despair. "And how do you want me to respond to *this*, Lord?" I asked out loud with anger in my tone. In the stillness I heard, "Be thankful in all circumstances, for this is God's will for you."

"Are you *kidding me*, Lord?" I yelled incredulously.

Somehow, it felt like God's presence began receding from the room. I knew I needed the Lord on my side through this, so, after a long silence, I muttered, "Thank you for allowing us to go through this." I didn't feel thankful, and I didn't want to. "Please make something good out of it," I said. "Thank you for being with us through this difficult situation." The more I prayed, the more my anger dissipated. I stopped gritting my teeth. God's peace floated into the room, surrounding me. Somehow, the Lord took my forced prayer of thankfulness and transformed it into genuine gratitude, and I sat in the living room far from alone.

Personal Action

Go find a quiet space where you can talk out loud, even if that just means standing in the bathroom for a few minutes. Think of a current painful situation or relationship. Thank God for allowing you to have that experience—out loud, even if it feels silly. It's OK if you have to grit your teeth, but try to keep your heart engaged. Thank him for the work he is doing through that experience. Thank him for how he is going to change you or others through it, for his presence in the midst of discomfort. Rack your brain for positive aspects of the experience, and continue thanking God aloud until you feel your heart soften.

When you're done, write down what you said and reflect on the experience of saying it aloud to God.

That day on the couch, in my anger and fear I did not feel thankful that God was allowing my family to go through such a difficult experience. But I chose to surrender to God's will, open my heart, and express thankfulness despite my emotions—and, much to my surprise, God used that act of obedience to draw me near to him and change my perspective.

Do you feel deeply thankful on a daily basis? For most of us, the answer is no. Gratitude may never have come naturally for us, or, if it did, we've lost it over the years to entitlement or hopelessness.

I should state clearly that thankfulness is the same thing as praise, the same thing as worship. These are all words we use to describe expressing admiration and appreciation to God for his goodness. Thus, thankfulness is foundational to Foundational Living and Parenting. You see, it is not possible to parent foundationally from an ungrateful heart, because thankfulness is central to a healthy relationship with the Lord. Ungratefulness reveals a heart that does not truly believe God is good, even if the mouth espouses it weekly. And if you do not have a healthy relationship with a good Father, how can you possibly lead your child in developing one?

Personal Reflection

Describe a difficult period in your life when you doubted God's goodness.

Looking back on that season, do you see God's goodness in the midst of the hardship? How did something good come from that time?

Check your heart: right now, do you believe God is good? It's OK if you question it, feel anxiousness or resistance. Share your feelings with the Lord.

If you feel anxiousness, use the space below to identify where those feelings are coming from.

The choice to focus on thankfulness so early in this workbook is an intentional one. The weeks to come are going to be challenging. I'm going to push you to reevaluate your priorities, examine your life story, and learn self-control in tense situations. In the very next section, we're going to take practical steps to bring your schedule in line with God's will and develop a devotional time that works for you. So why talk about thankfulness now?

Because thankfulness will change your heart and the way you see your world and the people, experiences, and possessions in it. Establishing a habit of thankfulness now will draw you nearer to God and equip you to see your priorities more clearly. It will soften your heart so you can feel God's love and goodness to you, allowing you to respond to others in a loving way.

There is only one way to foster a thankful life: choose it, even when you don't feel like it. It's true that thankfulness is our expression of already knowing God is good. But thankfulness is also the practice by which we learn to believe God is good. God built you. He knows how you work better than you do. His instruction to be thankful in all circumstances is not just a command to be polite. It's a revelation of the path that leads to his presence.

PARENTING TIP

Make thankfulness a family value by saying thankful prayers at dinnertime and bedtime.

Personal Reflection

Take a few minutes to practice being thankful in a variety of circumstances. Write at least one sentence thanking God for:

1. Something about each of your children

2. A characteristic you love about your spouse or significant other, if you're in a relationship

3. Something good about your job or your spouse's job

4. Something your parents or guardians did well

5. A valuable trait in at least one close friend

6. Something about your home

7. Something great about your city or community

Practicing thankfulness not only teaches us to believe God is good, but revolutionizes our relationships with the people around us. We become more positive and pleasant to be around, and the people in our lives respond to that. This is especially true in a marriage, where we often take one another for granted or focus on our spouse's shortcomings.

Now, don't get me wrong—it's not that you just need a better attitude and everything will be A-OK. You are not the only one who needs to change or is capable of change. If your boss is cruel, you don't have to ignore her slights and feign thankfulness for her offenses. If you're a stay-at-home mom, you are not expected to pretend that whatever your husband does is OK because he provides for you. No. I challenge women to thankfulness because it releases God's divine power in your life, leading to widespread change—real change—in you and in your relationship with your spouse, friends, family members, colleagues, authority figures, and the Lord.

Personal Action

Name one person in your life who you've felt frustrated with lately.

Write three things about that person you can be thankful for.

The next time you see this person, tell them one thing you appreciate about them.

A few years ago, Don and I hosted a Ugandan man named Peter for a few days, and he told me one of the most amazing stories about thankfulness I've ever heard.

Peter was a pastor in a southern city in Uganda, and some years earlier he'd felt the Lord call him north into territory dominated by a militant group known for kidnapping and turning children into soldiers. As he drove northward, he counted dozens of vehicles left in the ditch, clearly peppered with bullet holes. Pedestrians and drivers rushed down the road in the opposite direction with fear in their eyes. Suddenly, armed soldiers rushed out of the brush and surrounded his car. "I couldn't look to the right or the left or fear would overtake me," he said. "I had to look straight ahead and praise the Lord." He should have been dragged from the car and killed, but he wasn't. Instead, as Peter praised the Lord, peace washed over him and the soldiers slowly parted from his path.

Now *that* is giving thanks in all circumstances.

Personal Action

Read Psalm 23. Pause for a minute and then read it a second time. Let it sink deep into your soul.

Do you feel peace wash over you as you read Psalm 23? Even if you don't, can you sense the peace David felt as he wrote it? This is the peace David knew in the midst of being hunted by his enemies. This is the peace Peter experienced surrounded by soldiers that day on the road. This is the peace available to you every day, even when life around you is stressful or unfulfilling. You need only tap into it. Thank the Lord. Praise the Lord. Notice and know his goodness.

My son survived open-heart surgery, and today he is thriving. But what if he hadn't? What if the Lord had washed me with peace that day on the couch, only to allow my son's death one month later? Though I am fortunate enough not to have lost a child, I am no stranger to the reality of such tragedy. Too many of my dear friends have lost a child.

What does thankfulness look like for them? I can assure you it does not mean smiling up at the Lord, happy for the loss. Their grief has been debilitating. But these friends, who embody Foundational Living, see hope and beauty in the small things. They are thankful for the daily presence of divine comfort. They praise God for his unimaginable master plan. The perseverant gratitude I see in these families gets at the heart of what it means to live thankfully: that in all things, big and small, we look to God and know that he is good.

Personal Action

Every day for the next month, write ten things you are thankful for in your journal. As you write, silently pray thanks to the Lord. You can make this list entirely random—things you experience or observe—or you can create categories to fill every day. For instance, you might always write two things about your kids, two things about your job, two things about your living environment, two things about your body, and two things about God. It's up to you.

Hold yourself accountable by texting or emailing your mentor each day this month to share a couple of your choices.

Rocket Prayer

"Lord, help me be thankful in this moment."

Do you remember the basics of a rocket prayer from the first chapter? A rocket prayer is brief, and it is a request for personal transformation, not change in someone else or in circumstance.

This little prayer for thankfulness is useful all throughout the day. Say this prayer when you step outside and it's raining or freezing cold. Say this prayer when a bill arrives in the mail. Say this prayer when your neighbor's dog won't stop barking and your kids do that thing that drives you crazy. This week, when you're tempted to complain or lash out, try saying this quick prayer instead.

Prayer of Response

Before you close this workbook for the rest of the week, take a few minutes to write a prayer of response to God. First, thank him for ways he has been good to you. Then, tell him what you're thinking and feeling as you process what you've learned.

Pass It On

This week, ask your little ones to draw a picture of something they're thankful for. When the kids are done, ask them about what they've drawn. Then, start a prayer and ask the kids to take turns thanking God for what they drew. If you can spare fifteen minutes, I recommend sitting down to color with your kids. Draw a picture of them or of the whole family, then participate in sharing the drawing and thanking God for what you drew.

Also, make a point of modeling your thankfulness aloud to your children. When you go outside and it's raining, tell them you're glad the trees are getting a drink. When your kids are disappointed their dad missed a soccer game because of work, make a comment about how thankful you are that he has a job. This helps your kids learn to look for the good things, too.

RIGHTING PRIORITIES

THREE WEEKS

In this section, our goal is to address deep heart issues that shape the way we live our daily lives, ultimately taking practical steps to put God back on the throne.

3

reflecting on your schedule

Seek the Kingdom of God above all else,
and live righteously, and he will give you everything you need.

MATTHEW 6:33

I've always been a high-energy doer, and about the time my youngest turned four, I really hit my stride as a do-it-all fulltime mom. All four kids were involved in sports, clubs, or play groups, and I had a myriad of my own commitments: homeschooling, leading a Bible study for teen girls, helping to launch a Christian school—not to mention all the normal household responsibilities. I was on the go from the time I woke in the morning until I dropped into bed at night.

During that season, I began slacking on my practice of tucking my youngest, Cavan, into bed at night. I just didn't have the time or emotional energy for him by the end of the day. One night in particular, I remember hearing his pleading voice call from his bedroom, "Mommy, would you tuck me in?" I cringed. I felt I needed to stay focused on housework. "I'm so sorry, Cavan," I said. "I have to work." In my exhaustion, I justified my action: *I'll lose time and momentum. The dishes and laundry won't get done, and I'll be behind on tomorrow's work.* A sweet voice softly called back, "It's OK. I wuv you, Mommy."

A couple of nights later, Cavan asked me, "Mommy, will you come and lay down next to me until I fall asleep?" I knew I would fall asleep before he did. I started to reply, "Honey, I have—" but he interrupted me. His tone was apologetic, like he didn't want me to feel guilty. "I know, Mommy, you have night work." He meant to comfort me, but his words pierced me. Why did I choose duties over spending precious bedtime moments with my son?

That night, I saw the truth: I was prioritizing productivity over relationship with my son. And in the months that followed, the Lord helped me see that not tucking Cavan in at night was a small part of a much, much larger problem.

Personal Reflection

Describe a time when your actions did not align with your core priorities.

In those days, my life looked pretty impressive. I worked hard, and I believed that all my work was selfless sacrifice for my children and for the Lord. But those piercing words—"I know, Mommy, you have night work"—marked the beginning of a season of change as the Lord revealed that all my work really wasn't so selfless after all.

The reality was that, deep down, I had begun to believe lies instead of holding fast to God's truth—and those lies had influenced my motivations and behaviors in significant ways. I'd begun to believe that I needed to be respected by other people in order to have value, which motivated me to be accomplished and impressive as a parent rather than focused on nannying the King's children. I'd begun to believe that my kids needed many opportunities and experiences in order to lead good lives, which prompted me to fill their schedules (and mine) with activities. I'd begun to believe that God loved me *because* I served him faithfully, which led me to serve his kingdom for the wrong reasons. All of this led me to be busy, busy, busy.

As the Lord revealed these realities to me, he called me to make real changes in my life—changes that defied those lies and refocused my life on the top priority: him. He called me to pull the kids out of their activities and to step back from my own commitments, including the things I considered kingdom service. It was deeply uncomfortable and wonderfully transformative. It reset my priorities in a way that forever changed my life.

In this chapter and the next, we're going to walk together through that same process. We all believe lies. Every one of us. And those lies direct our lives in more dramatic ways than we realize.

If our job is to raise the King's children for kingdom service, it's essential that we do our best to live by the King's truth.

This process is designed to be convicting. If you do it with an open heart and honest reflection, it will inevitably leave you with challenging emotions. Know that the point is not to make you feel guilty, though you may very well feel that way at first, and that's OK. I've been through this! Just know that God is not sitting on high wagging a finger at you. He is reaching a hand to you, inviting you to see yourself and the world through his lens. He is inviting you to live by his truth because he longs to see you thrive.

Personal Action

Pause for a minute of prayer. Ask the Lord to open your eyes and ears to his Spirit so you can see your own heart clearly.

Let's start by looking at the kinds of lies that creep in and take over our hearts. These lies fall into two big buckets: lies about self, and lies about God.

Lies about self trick us into believing our value comes from ourselves, and they tell us fulfillment can be found in happiness, security, and comfort. In the United States, these lies tell us to keep up appearances. *Be successful, be stylish, lose the baby weight, have it all together.* These lies tell us we'll only be loved if we're perfect or if others need us. These lies tell us our kids need to succeed by the world's standards, and that to succeed they need a high-quality education and well-rounded extracurriculars, starting at an early age. *If your kids fail, you fail.*

These days, society also connects your value to your busyness. Busyness has, in many ways, become the latest status symbol. *You're not doing enough.* And if we aren't successful enough, smart enough, athletic enough—whatever enough—these lies tell us we're inadequate. *You are not qualified to teach your child what he needs to know.* They whisper that we need security in order to be happy. *You need a big salary. You need the safest organic food and the safest gear for your kids.* They tell us that new stuff or fun activities will quench our dissatisfaction. They tell us that comfort will give us the rest we crave. *You need a glass of wine to relax at night.* These lies about self push us to strive—for more money, more accomplishments, more stuff, more beauty, more control, more comfort, more distraction, more something—and lead us to constantly compare ourselves to others.

Now, strollers with top safety ratings and beach vacations aren't inherently bad. Healthy food certainly isn't. The lie is that they are absolutely necessary. You do not need the most expensive stroller. You do not need to explore a new country. Let's take it a step further: You do not need to be happy. You do not need to be successful. You do not need to be comfortable, or secure, or respected, or any other state of being you think will fill you up.

You need Jesus.

Your kids need Jesus.

And that's it.

Personal Reflection

Write down any lies about self from the text that resonate with you.

Take a minute to pray that the Lord will reveal other lies about self you believe. What other lies, not included in the text, might be in the driver's seat of your life?

Lies about God give us a distorted view of who God is and how he relates to us. In our culture, these lies tell us that God, like America, values independence and self-sufficiency. *God helps those who help themselves.* They tell us the Lord will love us more if we work hard or support Christian causes, which leads us to focus more on winning his approval than investing in relationship. These lies whisper that God is an authoritarian party pooper. *If you let him reign, he won't let you have any fun.* They tell you God should defer to your worldview. *God wants you to be happy, so he should give you want you want.* They tell you God isn't really good, isn't really in control, isn't really working for your flourishing—and that, therefore, you really ought to take over the throne.

God *is* good. He *is* faithful. He *is* working for your flourishing, even if it doesn't look like you expected. He is all the good things you crave: love, joy, glory, security, peace, knowledge, perfection, uniqueness, power, and fulfilling relationship. And his Word makes clear again and again that he calls us to dependence, not self-sufficiency. To community, not individualism.

Personal Reflection

Write down any lies about God from the text that resonate with you and why.

Take a minute to pray that the Lord will reveal other lies about God you believe. What other lies, not included in the text, might influence your thinking?

Identifying the lies we believe can be incredibly challenging. They hide beneath layers of cultural expectations and self-justification. I thought all my productivity was good for my kids and good for me, and the culture validated that. For me to see the truth, the Lord had to intervene and show me what had gone wrong.

One of the most heartbreaking aspects of that season was realizing that not only had I deceived myself, but that I was inadvertently teaching my children to believe the same falsehoods. By busying myself and pushing them into a multitude of activities, I was instilling in them habits of restlessness and self-sufficiency. I was failing to teach them rest, to provide space for them to learn time management and grow their imaginations. By prioritizing productivity over relationship, I was teaching them to put more effort into accomplishment than relational intimacy. On some level, I was teaching them they could earn God's love by working hard to serve him. Our kids might not always listen to our words, but they are always watching and learning from our actions. They are learning from you right now.

So, you have a choice. Do you want good kids, or do you want godly kids? Do you want to be comfortable, or do you want your children to know the Great Comforter? The way you live reflects your answers far more accurately than the words you speak. And so, right now, we're going to spend time analyzing the way we live. Our goal is to assess the way we spend our time, explore our motivations for those choices, and reflect on how those motivations connect to deeper lies in our life that need to be dealt with.

Personal Reflection

In your journal, make a list of all your children's regular commitments, from tutoring to sports to play dates to monthly library events. Note how much time each activity consumes. I recommend making two lists: one for weekly commitments, such as soccer practice and preschool, and one for less regular activities, such as the average time spent at birthday parties or play dates. As you make this list, say a rocket prayer of thankfulness over each item, showing appreciation to the Lord for the privileges that allow your kids to be part of these things.

Next, take notes about how you structure time for your children outside of those scheduled commitments. Be as specific as you can about how they spend free time. For instance, include the average time spent watching television, playing outside, reading, visiting places around town, etc.

Good job. Halfway there! Next, make a list of all your own scheduled commitments, from work to Bible study to monthly haircuts to organizing school fundraisers. Again, say a prayer of thankfulness for each item.

Finally, take notes on how you spend the remainder of your personal time. How much time do you spend cooking, cleaning, or doing laundry? Responding to emails? Playing with the kids? How much time do you spend reading or watching TV? How much time do you spend with the Lord? Try to be honest and accurate, even if it's not flattering.

Some of you are feeling exhausted right now. Your lists are lengthy, and your brains are tired from keeping all this information straight. Others of you are staring at short lists, wondering why you feel anxious when you really don't have much to do—and perhaps you're chastising yourself for not doing more. Whatever your inner critic is whispering to you, tell her to hush. We'll come back later to things that need to change.

Our next step is to explore the motivations behind our time management. This is hard work, and it requires honesty and critical self-awareness. When God began revealing the truth about my busyness, I was horrified by the selfishness in my own motivations. Did that mean I didn't love my children and love the Lord? Of course not! It simply meant that, like all human beings, I had a tendency to put myself first. As you reflect, know that I don't doubt for one second that you love your children unconditionally and sacrifice so much for them. After all, you're doing all the hard work in this book in order to be an even better mother to them.

Personal Reflection

Look over the two lists that describe how you have your children spend their time. Take one minute to pray that the Lord would help you see your heart clearly. Then, in your journal, begin writing any and all motivations that describe why you make those choices. Some motivations might span all the activities, while others will be specific to certain commitments. Here are a few ideas to get you started:

- "My kids drive me crazy when they are bored at home."
- "I'm too exhausted to organize structured activities at home."
- "I miss my kids too much when they're gone."
- "I want my kids to succeed in life."
- "My child asked to participate in this and enjoys it."
- "I want my kids to learn lessons or skills I can't teach them at home."
- "I don't like sports, so I'd rather my child not get into them either."
- "I feel bad that their dad is not around, so I compensate by giving them as much as I can."
- "I don't want to spend time driving my kids to and from activities."
- "Signing kids up for a variety of activities is what's expected of good moms these days."

Next, do the same with regard to your own time. Don't forget to say a prayer first. You need the Lord's help! Here are a few ideas to get you started:

- "I deserve something that's fun for me."
- "I don't have a choice—we need the money."
- "I don't want to be tied down by commitment."
- "It gives me the energy I need for the rest of my day."
- "I feel like God called me to this."

- "I'm just too tired to be involved."
- "I don't want to be irrelevant."

Our motivations reveal a lot about us and about our core beliefs, both true and untrue. Even the most innocuous motivations, such as wanting your kids to be successful or doing your duty, are often the tip of deeper lie icebergs. For instance, let's say you're super involved in your small church. You lead a Sunday school class for first graders, host a Bible study, participate in every church community event, and volunteer to type up and format the bulletin each week. You tell yourself you work so hard because it's selfless and the right thing to do. But, if you look at your heart honestly, your true motivation might be that you're afraid of being irrelevant in the community. You want to matter, to be needed. Dig deeper, and you can trace that motivation back to core lies that you believe about self: that your worth comes from what you can offer, and that people (and perhaps God) won't truly love you if you aren't needed.

Let's tackle a harder one—one that might be sensitive for some of you. Let's say your main motivation for enrolling your kids in numerous activities is that you and your spouse work full time, and therefore they need somewhere to be. How could there be anything wrong with that at a heart level? For some of you, there's nothing wrong. You have no choice but to work full time in order to provide the necessities for your family, or perhaps the Lord has called both of you to a certain kind of full-time work. But that motivation can also sprout from lies. Do you both work full time so your family can afford a big house, nice cars, regular vacations, and an abundance of toys? There might be a lie behind that, telling you that your kids need those nice things more than they need quality time with you. Do you work full time because a successful career is important to you, or because you wouldn't enjoy being a stay-at-home mom? There might be untruths behind that, too, telling you your worth is in your success or that you're selling yourself short by staying home with the kids.

Personal Reflection

Take a few minutes to pray. Ask the Lord to help you see any motivations or deeper lies you have missed before moving on to these questions. Write them here.

Consider your list of motivations. How do these motivations connect to deeper lies in your life?

Spend a few minutes journaling about how those core lies have shown up over the course of your life.

Now, spend several minutes journaling about how those lies have affected your family.

PARENTING TIP:

Try to understand what lies might be at play in your kids' hearts. For example, if your son keeps begging to join new sports teams when he doesn't actually seem to enjoy sports, he might believe he needs to be athletic in order to be liked.

In the next chapter, we will move into a time of repentance—that is, turning away from the lies we've believed and embracing the King's truth. Now, none of us are going to conquer these issues instantly. Cavan is all grown up, and sometimes I am still tempted by the desire for respect from my peers. If I'm not careful, I could slip back into a pattern of trying to earn my worth. But we can strip these lies of their power by choosing to refocus our lives on truth and reinstate God on the throne. We can make practical changes to reject their control over us, even if our hearts aren't totally on board yet.

In the meantime, there is heart work to do. Seeing how core lies shape our motivations and behaviors is painful. It can shatter our sense of self. Some of you may be feeling defensive and unwilling to see the ugly truth. Some of you might feel fearful, ashamed, or exposed. Throughout this week, keep a conversation going with God about this. Even if you're as busy as I was as a young mom, you can always find a few minutes for prayer each day. It's OK if it's while you're driving, cleaning, or taking a shower. Confess the lies you believe to God, and ask him to reveal the ones you don't yet see. Share with him how you're feeling—even if it's defensive or angry. He can handle it. Ask him to give you the wisdom you'll need to make necessary changes in your life. Ask him to help you believe the truth about yourself and about him, your King. By inviting the Lord to speak into this conversation about lies, you are taking important steps toward living in the truth.

Personal Reflection

During the week, come back here to take notes on these conversations with God. What has he revealed to you? How has your heart changed over the last few days?

At this point, do you feel the Lord calling you to take actionable steps, such as stepping back from a commitment or engaging in something you've resisted? If so, list those here as they come to mind.

Rocket Prayer

"Lord, I give you my heart."

Say this prayer in the morning when you rise and face a new day. Say this prayer when you feel defensive about the concepts in this chapter or guilty about the lies that have been motivating your behavior. Say this prayer when you start worrying about the changes we're going to talk about next week. The Lord is excited to meet you in this, and all he asks for is your heart.

Prayer of Response

Before you close this workbook for the rest of the week, take a few minutes to write a prayer of response to God. First, thank him for ways he has been good to you. Then, tell him what you're thinking and feeling as you process what you've learned.

Pass It On

This week, consider inviting your kids into what you've learned by taking a heart-level approach to discipline.

Just like us, our kids believe lies—even when they are very young. One major lie for young kids is that they are the center of the universe. The next time your child snatches a toy from someone else's hands, invest a couple of extra minutes in helping your child not only learn better behavior, but actually turn his heart toward truth. For instance, your side of the conversation might look like this: "Hey, Charlie, I saw you knock down Arabella's tower, and I want to talk to you about that. Why did you do that? I understand—knocking down towers can be fun. If you were building a tower and Arabella knocked it down, how would you feel? So if you feel sad when people knock down your towers, how do you think Arabella feels when you knock down her tower? I think you're right. What do you need to do to make it right? That's right. How about you go tell her you're sorry now? And maybe you can help her rebuild that tower." Finish with a hug and a reminder that you love him. This approach not only fixes the bad behavior, but helps your child learn a new truth: that his sister has her own unique feelings and sees the experience differently than he does.

If your children are old enough to read, consider turning the basic principles of this week's lesson into an art project. Draw a line down the center of a blank poster. On the left, write "LIES," and ask your kids to help you come up with lies they believe about themselves and about God. On the right, write "TRUTH," and invite your kids to help you identify the truth. For instance, if the lie is that "God only loves us if we're good," the truth is that "God loves us for who we are, not what we do." Tape this poster up as a reminder in your house, ideally somewhere that only members of your family will see it for the sake of your kids' privacy.

4

making changes

This world is fading away, along with everything that people crave.
But anyone who does what pleases God will live forever.

1 JOHN 2:17

In the first weeks following my conviction over Cavan's bedtime, I attempted to make small changes to straighten out my priorities. I committed to doing a bedtime routine with Cavan even if there were household chores waiting for me, and I tried to prioritize other relationship-building moments with my kids. But here's the thing: I didn't actually give up any of my busyness in order to make more time for relationships. Instead, I continued to lead that Bible study for teen girls, serve on the board of the new Christian school we'd helped launch, attend a moms' prayer group, and so on and so on—all while pushing myself to get it together and make time for relationship-building, too. In short, I was attempting to make small changes on my own terms rather than actually giving my schedule to the Lord.

Personal Reflection

Consider what you learned about yourself and your schedule last week. If you were going to make changes on your own terms instead of the Lord's, what might you tweak?

One cold, rainy day a couple of weeks later, I was driving my oldest daughter to an early morning basketball practice. It was just the two of us in the car—a valuable opportunity to focus on her and build our relationship. But what was I doing? Sitting silently, mentally absorbed in the day's to-do list: *I need to get their uniforms washed for their upcoming tournament. I need to arrange for someone to watch the dogs, and I need to get food to take to the games this weekend. I will run by the grocery store right after dropping Danae off, then drop the kids off at school by 8:00 a.m., before the prayer group starts. Oh—I'm supposed to bring cupcakes for Cammy's class party today. I'll add that to my grocery list.* My mind was so consumed with my own busy schedule that when Danae spoke to me, I didn't register a word she said. I'm not sure I realized she was speaking until she leaned my direction and said, "Mom?"

My gut twisted—just like it had a couple weeks earlier at Cavan's bedtime, when he'd sweetly called, "I know, Mommy, you have night work." After I dropped Danae at practice, I kept dwelling on a frightening thought: in ten years, she would be out of our home and living her own life. How would she remember me? As a mom who didn't pay attention to her? I didn't want that, but clearly my schedule was creating that kind of dynamic. I knew there would be consequences if I continued living this way, but I didn't like the idea of making real changes. In my head, I imagined that things would somehow be magically different in the future. *Sure,* I thought, *I'm swamped right now, but that's just unavoidable. Once we get through this phase, things will be different.* I knew it was a fantasy. Unless I did something to make change, the habits I had then would be even more entrenched ten years later.

The same is true for you. Whether you're a busy bee or a couch potato, your life won't change unless you surrender it all to the Lord and make changes according to his will. In the previous chapter, we uncovered deep lies about self and about God that are shaping how you spend your time and energy. In this chapter, we're going to work together to make practical changes that recenter your life on God and his vision for your days. To start, let's consider the consequences if you *don't* make changes.

> **PARENTING TIP**
>
> *Whenever you are, be all there. Put your phone down, ignore your to-do list, and choose to engage with your children.*

Personal Reflection

First, briefly revisit the previous chapter and look over the lies and motivations you uncovered. Then, come back and consider what the answer to these questions would be if you don't make any changes to your life.

MAKING CHANGES / 39

When your kids' college or adult friends ask what their mom was like, how will they describe you?

In ten years, what will your relationship with your spouse look like?

Adding ten years to a situation is a great tool for evaluating situations and behaviors. For example, add ten years to your daughter's hilarious lying habit. It could be a big problem when she's fifteen.

In ten years, what kind of relationships will you have with friends? What about with your church, neighbors, or other key members of your community?

In ten years, will you have responsibly stewarded the finances God has given you?

In ten years, what will your relationship with the Lord look like?

That day in the car with Danae I felt like the Holy Spirit poked me in the gut. I had tried to make changes, but doing things my way clearly wasn't working. Looking back on this story, I'm reminded of what Paul says in Romans 7:19: "I want to do what is good, but I don't. I don't want to do what is wrong, but I do it anyway." My sin nature was ruling me, and shallow tweaks weren't enough. My busyness was a reflection of my nature, of the lies I believed, and it was robbing me of the good things God wanted in my life. If my time management was really going to change, I needed to hand it over to God. After a few days of prayer and reflection, I closed my eyes and made a commitment: *I'm sorry, Lord. I have again let activities overshadow relationships. I have held onto control of my schedule. Starting now, you get to call the shots in my entire schedule. I want to reflect your nature, not mine. I want you to have all of me.*

Personal Reflection

What fears or concerns do you have about letting God call the shots when it comes to your time management?

How do those fears or concerns connect to lies you believe about self or about God?

Matthew 4:19 says, "Come, follow me." Follow now—without hesitation, negotiation, or arguing. Follow with your whole self—body, soul, and mind. He wants us to be all in. So, with that short prayer, I went all in. No more organizing my days based on my own beliefs about what was good for me, my family, and God's kingdom. It was time to base my days on *his* truths. It was time to live by the prayer I'd said for years: "Thy will be done on earth as it is in heaven."

And let me tell you, God sure had some changes in mind. Between prayer and conversations with my husband, the Lord quickly made it clear he was calling me to take drastic steps. He didn't just ask me to forfeit an activity here or there. He asked me to stop everything, at least temporarily—even Bible studies and prayer groups. He asked me to spend my time with him instead. And so, one by one, I backed out of all my commitments. I even stopped homeschooling and pulled my kids out of sports for that season.

It was humiliating. My identity had been wrapped up in being worthy of respect, and backing out of my commitments made me feel like a failure. The Lord had slowly been revealing to me the lies I believed about self and about him, but this process made me face them in a whole new way. I struggled with feelings of boredom, shame, and purposelessness. But with time, the Lord began to transform my heart. Instead of finding my worth in what others thought about me, I began to find my identity in the Lord. And instead of needing activities to make me feel accomplished and purposeful, I learned to rest and find meaning in God alone. I learned to reject the lies that had dominated my life and embrace the truth in their place.

Now, let me break for a caveat: I don't believe the Lord is necessarily going to call you to make such dramatic changes. Please don't be scared away by my rather extreme experience. You go-getters won't all be asked to cancel every engagement, and all of you homebodies won't be asked to kick it into high gear. I don't know what the Lord has in mind for you. It could be radical. It could be slight. I do know that whatever it is, it's in your best interest.

So, are you willing to let the Lord call the shots? Is it time to live by his will, not yours? Will you deny the lies you believe by letting God rule your life according to his truth?

Personal Reflection

Are you willing to make this commitment, even if you don't know yet what the Lord will ask of you?

If the answer is yes, take a moment to pray. Tell the Lord you're ready to follow him with your days. Ask him to help you clearly understand what he wants you to do, and pray that he'll help you take the hard steps.

If you're having trouble surrendering your time and energy to the Lord, take a few days to pray and talk to your mentor before moving forward in the workbook.

So, what does it look like to begin this process in your own life?

In short: prayer. At the end of the previous chapter, you were encouraged to keep the conversation going with the Lord by talking with him each day about the lies you were processing, the feelings of defensiveness or anxiety that might creep in, and the wisdom you'd need for taking next steps. If you've been praying about all this, I hope the Lord has begun to at least hint at changes he'd like you to make in your life.

If you're feeling totally lost, without any idea what the Lord is calling you to do, I encourage you to close the workbook and take a few days to ponder and pray. Ask the Lord to make his will clear to you. Here's a short prayer you might say a couple times each day: "Lord, I want to live by your truth. Help me know how to challenge the lies in my life by changing the way I spend my time. I'm ready to make changes according to your will."

Personal Reflection

List any changes to your schedule you are confident the Lord wants you to make, whether it's adding or subtracting activities.

List any changes you're wondering about or exploring as possible calls from God.

Whether you know exactly what needs to change or are simply rolling some ideas around in your mind, I encourage you to open up communication with members of your family. After all, some of the changes God calls you to make will have big implications for them. If you're married, tell your husband about what you've been learning, and share with him your desire to follow God's will for your time. Consider inviting him to pray with you or discuss possible changes. Who knows, maybe the Holy Spirit has been pestering him about the family's time, too. If your kids are old enough, loop them in as well. Tell them you want to center your life and the family life around God, and that it might mean making some changes to the schedule soon. Be sure to articulate the intention behind it all. You're not just switching things up because you want to. You're making changes because God, who is on the throne in your life, is asking you to.

I'm lucky to have the family I have. When I told Don I wanted to give my schedule over to God, he was actually the first one to say out loud that he thought I needed to give up all my commitments for the time being. When I shared the details with the kids, they were wonderfully supportive, even though it meant giving up the sports they loved for a season.

While I pray your families respond with encouragement and support, I realize that will not be the case for many of you. If your husband is achievement-oriented, he may not like the idea of seeing you cut back. If he's easily overwhelmed, he might be resistant to you taking on new commitments. I cannot speak to every marriage dynamic, so I simply encourage you to pray and talk with your mentor. She can offer advice based on your unique situation.

If your kids give you trouble, I encourage you to be firm, but have sympathy. You'd be bummed and irritated if an authority figure took away your dance class, too. Keep coming back to the big picture: this is about living life the way God wants, because what God wants is always best for us—even if it doesn't feel like it in the moment. Remind them that the change isn't necessarily permanent. After a season of quiet, the Lord freed me to re-enroll my kids in sports and reestablish some of those original personal commitments. The difference was that it was God making the decision, not me.

Personal Reflection

Write a prayer for your family. What do you hope God does in your family as a whole through the changes you're about to make?

Very soon it will be time to take action—send emails, place phone calls, do what it takes to make changes. But many of you might be struggling with doubt or anxiety. So, before we move into the action steps, let's address seven key mental hang-ups that might be getting in your way.

"I'm not a quitter." When Jesus called the disciples to follow him, they left a lot behind—families, jobs, maybe volunteer roles in the synagogue or the neighborhood. Were they quitters? No. They just had something more important to do. If God is calling you to step back from a commitment, say no to worrying about your reputation. God is calling you to something else, and he thinks it's more important.

"I don't have the bandwidth to do more." If God is calling you to make new commitments or engage with your community in an uncomfortable way, he will give you the energy you need.

Perhaps he knows you'll get a surprise energy lift from spending more time with other people. Or maybe he's just asking you to trust that he'll provide.

"The work has to get done." Nervous about backing out of your commitment to organize the annual school Valentine's party or lead worship at church because the show must go on? If the Lord is concerned about something getting done, he will find someone else to do the work. Who knows, maybe at the same time he's calling you to cut back your endeavors, he's calling someone else to engage more actively.

"This decision will hurt my family." Yes, others will be affected by your decision to be obedient to Christ. Think back to Jesus's disciples. When they left home to follow Christ, they left behind parents, families, and communities that depended on them. This left a need. Someone had to catch the fish for the family to survive. When God calls us to something, we can trust that he will care for those who are affected by our obedience. It may be the very thing that draws them to a closer walk with Christ.

"I need this outlet." The Lord knows what you need. If this is the best outlet for you, he will bring it back with deeper meaning and a new perspective. Or, he may open a new outlet that is an even better fit for you.

"I am doing a good thing. How can he want me to give it up?" God is much more concerned with our hearts than with our achievements on his behalf. Our heart needs to be in the right relationship with him first—and perhaps you need a break in order to get right with God on his terms. From there, he will lead you into the good things that are best for you and for your community.

"What will others think?" Scripture repeatedly calls us to value God's opinion over man's. This choice keeps him on the throne of your life.

Personal Reflection

Which of the thoughts above are you struggling with?

What other resistant thoughts do you have? Consider how the Lord would respond to each.

Take a moment to pray. Pour out your doubts and fears to the Lord. Ask him to take them and to give you his peace as you move ahead.

All right, ladies. The time has come. You've known since the start of the previous chapter that eventually you'd be asked to make real and serious changes to your calendar. Hopefully, you've been praying over this for at least a few days. If you're really struggling to discern what steps the Lord wants you to take in order to reflect his will in the way you spend your time and energy, please pause as long as you need. Pray over this and talk with your mentor. The point isn't just to make changes—it's to make the changes that God is asking of you. This is about giving your life and schedule to the Lord, whatever that looks like for you. Listen and follow him.

Personal Reflection

Name the changes God is calling you to make in the way you spend your time and energy.

How do these changes challenge the lies you believe about self and about God?

When God gives us instructions, it's important to obey fully and immediately. With this in mind, take several minutes to make a game plan for enacting these changes. For instance, if God is asking you to back out of the PTA, weekly happy hour, and playing piano for the kids' choir, make a note of who you need to call or email, and set a deadline for taking that step. Whenever possible, I strongly encourage you to set deadlines within the next week. This works the same way for those of you who will be adding activities to your calendar instead of subtracting them: note who you need to contact about getting together for dinner or signing up for a volunteer shift, and set a deadline.

I am proud of you for taking this step. It is a difficult thing to do, but you won't regret it. At least, not in the long run. Like me, you may struggle in the early weeks as you adjust to your new-found free time or—at the other end of the spectrum—settle into the new demands of a busier schedule. As hard as this phase is, you have taken steps down a path to contentment, fulfillment, and peace in your life.

Rocket Prayer

"Let my heart want nothing but you, Jesus."

Say this prayer when you get ready to call someone this week to cancel or sign up for a commitment. Say this prayer when you feel doubts creep up. Say this prayer when you worry what someone else—including your husband or children—will think about your decisions. You were designed to be fulfilled by the Lord alone, and he will delight in helping you get there.

Prayer of Response

Before you close this workbook for the rest of the week, take a few minutes to write a prayer of response to God. First, thank him for ways he has been good to you. Then, tell him what you're thinking and feeling as you process what you've learned.

Pass It On

Take time this week to tell your children about the changes that you are making and why. Maybe, as you tuck them into bed, share a little of your struggle and how you want to give control of your life to the Lord. This not only builds intimacy with your children and helps them understand changes that are happening, but models godly decision-making.

Beyond that, one key way to invite your children into what you've learned (and done) this week is to challenge them to surrender to a higher authority, too. If you have a toddler, sharing might be a good place to start. When you have an upcoming play date, talk with your child ahead of time about sharing her favorite toy with her friend. Tell her that sharing isn't just about being good—it's about doing what God says is best, even if it isn't what she wants. Even if she only obeys because you said so, she is surrendering self to a higher authority: her mom. Later, it will be the Lord.

If you have older children, consider inviting them to participate by evaluating their own time management. For instance, after sharing the changes you're making and how God called you to those changes, you might say, "You know, you can let God call the shots in your life, too. It isn't just for adults. Would you be interested in that?" Help them make a list of how they spend their time, then ask them what they think God might want them to do differently. If there's a certain activity you don't think is healthy—such as watching too much television—it's OK to subtly point your child to that. "What about TV time? Do you think God might have a better way for you to spend the afternoon?" Pray together, help your child arrive at a good decision, and then support your child in following through on his decision. For example, if your son wants to spend more time playing with the neighbor who just moved to town, help facilitate that.

5

new every morning

The LORD says,
"I will guide you along the best pathway for your life.
I will advise you and watch over you."

PSALMS 32:8

I still remember the restlessness I felt in those early days after cutting commitments from my schedule. I'd open the door to the house after dropping my children off at school and feel a wave of dread. The house was empty, and there was nothing pressing to accomplish. I felt lonely and unproductive. The Lord had called me to say no to all the activities that made me feel respected and important, and I was worried my life would be boring. The silence in the house was a reminder of the Lord's instructions: *spend your time with me.*

I'd been in the habit of reading Scripture regularly for years, but I'll be honest: it wasn't exactly the quality time I knew the Lord wanted. My time in Scripture was always rushed (a few quick verses in the morning out of duty) or driven by some kind of external agenda, such as preparing for Bible study. Rarely, if ever, did I simply hang out with the Lord by spending unhurried, agenda-free time in the Word. I knew that had to change. After all, the Lord had called me to correct my priorities. There's no way I could follow through completely without treating my relationship with the Lord as the most important relationship I had.

Personal Reflection

Be honest: when is the last time you spent unhurried, agenda-free time reading the Bible? The goal here isn't to feel guilty, but to be aware and honest with ourselves.

I decided to commit to devotional time every morning after taking my kids to school, when the house would be quiet. The first day, I sat in a chair by the window and forced myself to read my Bible. I tried hard to concentrate on the words and their meaning, but within a few minutes I found myself pacing the floor, restless and wanting to accomplish something. Frustrated, I sat back down and began reading and praying. My mind wandered to all the things I could be doing. Soon, without realizing it at first, I was up and pacing the floor again. This pattern continued for four agonizing weeks. I knew I was in a battle, and it had to be fought. God had to win out over self.

Over the course of several weeks, my soul started to settle down. I began to embrace the silence during devotional time, resting in the space it gave me to open my heart and listen. As I released any resentment I felt over giving up my schedule, contentment and peace flowed in. Eventually, I found myself genuinely sinking into this time, enjoying the Scriptures, and even feeling energized after each devotion.

I began to notice changes in the rest of my life, too. I was naturally more patient with my children, and I had more compassion toward others. I noticed the homeless men and women on street corners that I'd somehow never really seen before. I recognized my friends' needs even when they acted like everything was OK. My selfish nature was melting away, and I was beginning to see the world through God's lens.

Personal Reflection

Think about a time when you worked hard to change your habits. For instance, maybe you started exercising regularly, learned to eat healthier, or decided to quit smoking. What comes to mind?

Take a few moments to reflect on that process. What challenges did you face?

How has that change positively affected your life or your family's life?

The last couple of weeks have been challenging. You've analyzed your motivations and faced lies you believe about self and about God. You've made a commitment to correct your priorities—putting God's truth above your beliefs, his will for your time above your own preferences.

You didn't do all this for a nebulous "something better." You did it because God is your King, and his rightful place is on the throne. Because a life in love with Jesus is far better than a life that's accomplished or comfortable. Because you're ready to stand on something solid.

In this chapter, we're going to take the next step toward making the Lord the center of our lives by learning to spend time with him each day. Like changing your food choices or learning to exercise regularly, establishing a habit of daily time in Scripture is a challenging process. Rest assured that you're not expected to be perfect. You're only expected to begin.

Note: If you're already in the habit of reading and spending unhurried time with the Lord every day, good for you! Parts of this chapter may not feel relevant, but I encourage you to still read it. You might find a nugget that enhances your connection with the Lord.

Personal Reflection

How do you feel about starting a practice of daily devotion?

If this stirs up negative emotions, such as irritation or nervousness, take a few minutes to journal about that. Where do those feelings come from?

For many, the thought of reading the Bible daily stirs up some unpleasant feelings—and that's OK. Many of us carry some baggage in this area. Perhaps you've repeatedly tried and failed to start this habit, and now the thought just makes you feel guilty. Maybe in the past you've maintained this habit, but stopped because it felt dead and dry. Consider this chapter an opportunity to start fresh and start right.

Personal Action

Take a few minutes to pray through any negative feelings. God can handle the truth, so tell him what's on your mind. Ask him to take away your guilt, shame, and fear.

Spending time with the Lord isn't something we *should* do because we're Christians. It's a privilege we're invited into. The King and Creator of the universe wants to have a deep relationship with us, and that's amazing. But simply believing he exists isn't enough to create relationship. Neither is listening to others talk about him, nor asking for things every once in a while. Just like with any human being, we have to actually visit with God regularly in order to get to know him.

That's what daily devotion is. It's quality time—the same kind you know is essential to your human relationships. It's the way you build friendships, the way you fall in love.

Personal Reflection

Think back to the beginning of your most significant romantic relationship, and consider the statements below. Which ones were true for you as you fell for this person?

_____ You adjusted your schedule in order to spend time with him.

_____ You thought about him when he wasn't around.

_____ You tried new foods or activities because he enjoyed them.

_____ You were acutely aware of where he was and what he was doing.

_____ You just wanted to be with him, even if you weren't doing something you'd normally enjoy.

_____ You were eager to hear his perspective on everything.

_____ You began to care about the people and interests he cared about.

The Bible describes Jesus as our groom. He's our spouse, our lover, our partner for life—not some distant being who watches over us. We are called to love him, know him, make time for him, listen to his perspective, care about what he cares about. He asks us to try new things, to know what he's up to, to remember him always. And the way to get there, of course, is to spend time with him and get to know him intimately.

So, what does this quality time look like? Well, I believe healthy devotional time is unhurried, God-focused, agenda-free, and happens near the start of the day.

Unhurried: No visit is a good visit if you're in a hurry to get it over and done with. Even if your devotional time is only ten minutes, open your heart and be fully present during that time.

God-focused: Healthy devotional time is about getting to know the Lord—not extracting an application for yourself. Approach your devotional time with curiosity about God's personality and perspective.

Agenda-free: Reading Scripture as homework for Bible study or a Religion 101 course doesn't really count as healthy devotional time. Can you get to know God better through those readings? Of course! But I'd like to see you aim for quality time that's entirely voluntary.

Near the start of the day: It's during devotional time that God energizes you, encourages you, and helps you see the world through his lens. The earlier you meet with him, the earlier you benefit from having that special boost the rest of the day.

The specifics are up to you. You can use some kind of devotional guide or simply work your way through a book of the Bible. You can commit to thirty minutes or five minutes. You can do it before you get out of bed in the morning, or you can sit down with coffee and a snack.

> **PARENTING TIP**
>
> *Consistency isn't only important in forming your own habits. It's key in shaping your kids' hearts and minds, too.*

Whatever you decide, here are some practical tips for making it happen:

Build a routine. Consistency is key to changing your habits. Whether you have devotional time while nursing your baby, during quiet play after breakfast, or when the house is empty, try to keep it the same each day.

- **Prepare ahead of time.** Do yourself a favor and take some small practical steps to make this devotional time easier. If you're rising extra early, set your coffee maker to have a mug ready for you when you wake. If you plan to read Scripture while you feed an infant, make sure your Bible—and a bookstand, if you need it—are within reach of your favorite nursing spot.
- **Start your day right.** Set your alarm to play worship music, and put an index card on your bedside table with a short, written prayer to read before your feet touch the floor. If you tend to reach for your phone first thing, set your lock screen to a favorite Bible verse. These small connections with Jesus will help you follow through on a deeper devotional time—whether it's ten minutes or two hours after you first wake.

Personal Reflection

Take a minute to pray. Ask God what he thinks is the best idea for your devotional time.

Now, make a plan. When are you going to have your daily devotional time? What practical steps do you need to take ahead of time to make it work?

Several years ago, a dear friend named Mel chose to establish a daily devotional routine in her busy life, and I'll never forget the dedication she showed. At the time, her boys were about four and six. She was a full-time elementary teacher, and her workload was heavy. In addition to work and parenting, she was taking night classes to earn a master's degree.

Mel was swamped. She rose early every day and took her sons to two different schools before work. Since her husband had a long commute and didn't get home until after dinner, Mel was responsible for shuttling her children to and from appointments, play dates, and sporting events before taking care of dinner, chores, and helping the kids with homework. After her boys were in bed, she corrected her students' papers and did her own schoolwork. She rarely made it to bed before midnight.

Mel, of all people, did not have extra minutes in her day for unhurried time with the Lord. Nevertheless, she started setting her alarm an hour earlier than usual—long before the sun rose. She would build a fire in the woodstove and begin each morning with prayer and Scripture.

Mel is not a morning person. Yet she insists that she would not be able to sustain her lifestyle without her early morning devotional time. Somehow, she says, choosing the Lord over sleep has resulted in more energy, more efficiency, and a better attitude each day.

PARENTING TIP

Your children need quiet time, too. Even if they don't nap anymore, they can rest and recharge by taking a break to read, think, or play quietly in their room.

I share this story with you for two reasons. First, to challenge you. If Mel can make time for a devotional hangout with God, so can you. You are not too busy. Second, I share it to encourage you. Mel's story shows what a difference a morning devotional can make in the rest of life. Because Mel spent time with the Lord early in the day, she was able to stay connected to him all day long. Not only did that mean she had a deeper and more fulfilling relationship with her King, but it gave her more energy, more efficiency, and more patience to sustain an overwhelming lifestyle. Without all-day support from the Lord, Mel would have burned out.

That last point is key: the whole purpose of having this devotional time in the morning is so you can stay connected with him all day long. It's not a box we check off. It's the opener to an all-day conversation. Habits like morning devotions, saying rocket prayers, and practicing thankfulness provide a framework for continued connection. These habits are life changing, because they turn our face toward God in all circumstances. Whether we're asking for patience when our child makes a mess or thanking God for a rainstorm, we're looking at him instead of ourselves.

Personal Reflection

Take a few minutes to brainstorm ways you can continue the conversation with God throughout the day. To get you started, here are a few ideas: listen to worship music while you cook, set a reminder on your phone to find something to be thankful for, or process a challenging situation with the Lord while you shower.

Before we wrap up, let's consider a few mental roadblocks you might hit as you try to establish this new routine. For me to enjoy my coffee dates with the Lord, I had to work through some deeply ingrained habits and bad attitudes, and the same will likely be true for you. Based on my own experience, here are some unhelpful thoughts that might crop up, along with some frank responses:

"I am too busy today!" Too busy to connect with the only one who can give you the help you need? The only one who can lead you to the best plan for your life? This doesn't make sense. If God is truly your king, you'll make time.

"I am bored!" Our Creator and Bridegroom is boring? Pray and ask God to help you lean into the quiet—especially if you're used to always being entertained. Ask him to reveal himself to you and help you see Scripture in a new way, because I assure you he is not boring.

"I am too tired—I can't keep my eyes open!" Your God has the power to keep you awake. Ask for it. Think of Mel, and trust that he can give you energy no matter how little sleep you got.

"I am not getting anything out of it." If you're approaching Scripture with the question, "What can I get out of this?" then you need to adjust your posture. Instead, ask "Who is God?" when you open your Bible. Pray the Lord will help you become a curious learner.

"I am getting distracted." Of course you're getting distracted. You're human. And, frankly, the Enemy is great at pulling our minds off God. Ask the Lord to give you focus, and make a choice to redirect your thoughts to him.

"I keep failing, so I might as well give up." The Lord isn't mad at you for missing a day (or days). His grace covers your insufficiency. Stop worry about your performance, and repent for missing your date with the Lord. Then, consider some practical changes that might help you stay on track.

Notice what all the above have in common: the word "I." These resistant thoughts make us the focus instead of God. We have to decide in advance we aren't going to allow self-centered thoughts to be obstacles to knowing the Lord.

Personal Reflection

Read Psalm 25, and take a moment to let the words wash over you.

Now, take a moment to consider those bad attitudes listed above. What are you going to say to yourself or God when those thoughts arise? Thinking about it now will help you respond effectively in the moment—especially if you'll be groggy from waking early.

As you begin your new routine this week, remember that it's a long process. Trust that the more of your heart you give to the Lord, the more connection, hope, and encouragement he gives back. The Lord created you for unhurried time with him. After all, you were designed for Eden.

Rocket Prayer

"Lord, show me how to know you better."

Say this prayer when you sit down to start your devotional time. Say it when you catch yourself distracted or exhibiting a bad attitude. Second Corinthians 3:16–18 says, "whenever someone turns to the Lord, the veil is taken away . . . and wherever the Spirit of the Lord is, there is freedom. So all of us who have had that veil removed can see and reflect the glory of the Lord." You need God in order to know God better, and he is more than happy to help.

Prayer of Response

Before you close this workbook for the rest of the week, take a few minutes to write a prayer of response to God. First, thank him for ways he has been good to you. Then, tell him what you're thinking and feeling as you process what you've learned.

Pass It On

If your children are old enough to play quietly on their own, allow them to witness your devotional time. Seeing you make time for the Bible each day teaches them it's normal and important. Make sure your kids know that Scripture and prayer is your top priority during that time. If they approach you with requests, ask them to wait until you are done: "Let's talk about that in a few minutes, OK? Right now Mommy is focused on spending time with God."

Also, establish a practice of reading the Bible and praying with your kids. You can do this as part of a bedtime routine or work it in somewhere else. Be consistent in prioritizing this time, even if things aren't going as planned. For instance, if you have a habit of reading the Bible together at night, don't skip this routine when your child is late for bed. What's more important: five extra minutes of sleep, or teaching your child that the Bible is a top priority?

It's also a good idea to teach your children how to have quiet time. Everyone needs quiet in their lives, and children are no exception. As they begin growing out of naps, institute a routine time for quiet play—even if it's only fifteen minutes long. Provide kids with books, audiobooks, quiet toys, and art supplies they can use on their own. Tell them only to come talk to you if there's an emergency (and clearly define what constitutes an emergency, based on their age and maturity). This time might be hard for kids, especially at first, but it will teach them the invaluable skill of entertaining themselves instead of depending on external stimulation.

RELATIONSHIP BUILDING

THREE WEEKS

Now that we've taken practical steps to place God on the throne of our lives, we will spend three chapters focused on growing our relationships with the King through trust, obedience, and surrender.

6

trust: perspective when life is difficult

Trust in the LORD with all your heart;
do not depend on your own understanding.
Seek his will in all you do,
and he will show you which path to take.

PROVERBS 3:5–6

Several years ago, after all four of my children were out of the house, Don and I hit a rough patch financially. With little to no money coming in, we slowly emptied our savings account to cover basic expenses. Eventually, the well ran dry, and we faced a month with no income, no leftover savings, no way to pay bills. I remember the day that scary reality hit me. I felt myself begin to panic. In my gut, I wanted to grab hold of every penny in the house—every bill, every coupon—and hold on tight. Instead, I took our golden retriever, Bingley, for a walk in the woods. I needed time alone to pray in God's creation.

Once we got beyond the residential area, I unclipped Bingley's leash and let him run. I smiled as I watched him happily dash from bush to bush, smelling traces of critters who had scampered away. I noticed that no matter how excited he got about a scent, he consistently came back to check in with me, making sure he was going the right direction, that I was with him. *He has no idea where we are going*, I thought, *he is just enjoying every moment*. Bingley knew I would take us on a good path—all he had to do was check in, listen, follow. He didn't have to be responsible for getting us home. His trust in me gave him freedom to do what dogs do. *I wish that kind of trust came naturally for me*, I thought. The beautiful simplicity of Bingley's example made me determined to practice trusting God like my dog trusted me. And that day, trusting God meant unclenching my fists and lifting my pennies, openhanded, to the Lord.

Personal Reflection

Describe an area of your life that you hold with clenched fists.

I am a classic worrywart. I worry about our money. I worry about the safety of my husband and children. I worry about the health of the tomatoes growing in the garden. Letting go of my fears about our finances was no easy task. When I felt myself beginning to fret or search for solutions, I prayed and confessed my worry, asking God to help me trust like Bingley. A week passed, and nothing happened. We paid for groceries with the credit card. A second week went by, then a third. We needed money. Within a few days we'd have to pay our mortgage, utility, and credit card bills.

Personal Reflection

Briefly name a few instances in your life when you endured an uncomfortable wait, such as a season of infertility, job searching, or awaiting college acceptance letters or medical test results.

How did you handle those seasons of waiting? Can you identify a pattern in your responses? (For instance, perhaps you carefully researched any related information, hoping to arm yourself with competence. Or maybe you assumed an apathetic attitude, thinking indifference would prevent hurt feelings or dashed hopes.)

Just before the end of the month, a knock came at the door. A UPS man needed a signature for a large envelope. I wasn't expecting anything, so I eagerly opened the folds. Inside was a short note saying, "Dear Don and Brenda, we love you! Just a small love-you gift!" It wasn't small. I almost couldn't breathe. Inside was a $5,000 check. Tears filled my eyes and awe washed over me. We hadn't even told these friends the details of our situation. The Lord had waited until the last second, giving me nearly four weeks to give up on him and problem solve my own way out of danger. But I didn't, and I couldn't take an ounce of credit for the money that came through.

Personal Reflection

Describe a time when the Lord came through for you in a surprising way.

If you can't think of an example, consider why. Have you always tried to problem solve your own way out of hard situations? Have you taken credit when the Lord was really the one in control?

Learning to look for God's follow-through takes practice and patience—sometimes a lot of patience. That month I spent waiting for his deliverance felt awfully long, but in the scheme of things it was a tiny blip. Often, the Lord works slowly over years, allowing pain and hardship to shape us as he carves a path. Think about the life of Joseph, whose story is told in the later chapters of Genesis. He was the favorite son of a wealthy man, and he probably had high expectations for the life ahead of him. Then, because of his brothers' jealousy, Joseph found himself a slave in a foreign city where he did not speak the language.

It's a drama you probably know well: Joseph's owner, Potiphar, was impressed with his new slave and put him in charge of everything he owned. Joseph kept his eyes on the Lord, served his master the best he could, and God blessed him in his work. Potiphar's wife was also impressed with Joseph and wanted him to sleep with her. When he refused, she took revenge by telling her husband Joseph tried to rape her. Understandably, Potiphar was furious and had Joseph thrown in prison. But even there, God blessed him and gave him favor in the eyes of his authorities, and the jailer put him in charge of taking care of other prisoners.

Because Joseph had frequent contact with the other prisoners, he got to know Pharaoh's cupbearer, who had been tossed into prison for offending the ruler. When the cupbearer had a strange dream, the Lord gave Joseph understanding to interpret its meaning, and his predictions came true. But when the cupbearer was reinstated, he forgot to tell Pharaoh about his friend who was wrongly imprisoned.

Two whole years passed before Pharaoh dreamed about seven cows and seven ears of corn and the cupbearer remembered Joseph. From there, things finally went uphill. Joseph was summoned from the dungeons to meet with Pharaoh, where he interpreted the dreams—and clearly insisted that it was the Lord's doing, not his own—and recommended that Pharaoh put someone in charge of preparing the nation for famine. Pharaoh hired Joseph on the spot, and the Lord blessed Joseph in his leadership. At the end of the story, of course, Joseph is reunited with his family after two decades away.

Looking at Joseph's story as a whole, you might say he lived a wonderful life. He was Pharaoh's right-hand man and he saved an entire region from starvation. He had wealth, children, a beautiful reunion with his parents and brothers, and a truly unforgettable legacy. But inspect the details of his days, and the horror is hard to imagine. His own brothers conspired to murder him. He was sold into slavery and walked to Egypt on foot. He spent years as another man's property. His reputation was destroyed and he was thrown into prison for a crime he didn't commit. He spent years in that prison. Yet he consistently kept his eyes on the Lord and behaved with integrity, despite having so many opportunities to do otherwise.

Just think—if Joseph had fought against his brothers when they wanted to sell him to the merchants, they would have opted for their original plan and simply killed him. If he had complained and resisted the merchants on the long journey to Egypt, he would have been badly beaten or maybe even killed—and certainly not sold to a top client like Potiphar. If Joseph had taken the opportunity to sleep with Potiphar's wife, he would have been put to death. If he had been bitter, rebellious, or resigned to apathy in prison, the jailer would not have appointed him to a leadership position, and he never would have met the cupbearer, and therefore never have been introduced to Pharaoh.

Despite Joseph's harrowing life circumstances, his attitude reflected an unshakable trust in the Lord. He gave thanks in all circumstances and consistently sought the Lord's will. He never once attempted to orchestrate an escape or take advantage of his authorities' trust in him. And because Joseph put one foot in front of the other on the path God laid out for him, he went on to save the lives of millions.

Personal Reflection

Read Proverbs 3:5–6.

Meditate on the first line: "Trust in the Lord with all your heart." Try rewriting this command in your own words.

Now, focus on the second line: "Do not depend on your own understanding." Think about the area of your life that you hold with clenched fists. What does your human understanding tell you about this area of life?

Read the third line again: "Seek his will in all you do." What would it look like for you to unclench your fists and seek the Lord's will?

Are you willing to defer to his will, even if you don't yet know what it is? If so, make a commitment by writing "Yes, Lord!" below.

If you answered yes, copy the fourth line in your own handwriting: "He will show you which path to take." This is his promise to you if you trust him.

It is easy to look at the bad circumstances in our lives—from a broken washing machine to a floundering marriage—and sink into despair. It's easy to become bitter, to become controlling, to slump into apathy. Yet we must remember that God has a plan and a purpose, and if we trust him and seek his will, he will light up the next few feet of the path. He has not failed his people before, and he's not going to start now. In John 16:33, Jesus tells us that "here on earth you will have many trials and sorrows"—a guarantee that each of us will encounter hardship. And what does he say next? "But take heart, because I have overcome the world."

Sometimes, even though I know all this, I still get stuck and sink into worry and gloom. I find that even if I believe truths about God in my head, they don't always sink permanently into my heart. And so, with time, I've come up with a system for dealing with my own heart in those seasons: seven questions that lead me to a place of trust.

Personal Tool

The next time you face difficult circumstances, work through these seven questions in order, reading the accompanying Scripture and praying through the answer to each one. If you get stuck on one and don't feel like you can honestly assert the truth, stay on it for as long as you need. You may need to read and pray through that question for days or even weeks until your heart softens.

1. Does God love me?
   - The faithful love of the LORD never ends! . . . Great is his faithfulness; his mercies begin afresh each morning. (Lamentations 3:22–23)
   - Can anything ever separate us from Christ's love? Does it mean he no longer loves us if we have trouble or calamity, or are persecuted, or hungry, or destitute, or in danger, or threatened with death? . . . Despite all these things,

overwhelming victory is ours through Christ, who loved us. And I am convinced that nothing can ever separate us from God's love. Neither death nor life, neither angels nor demons, neither our fears for today nor our worries about tomorrow—not even the powers of hell can separate us from God's love. (Romans 8:35–38)

2. Did God know this was going to happen?
   - You know everything I do. You know what I am going to say even before I say it, Lord. You go before me and follow me. You place your hand of blessing on my head. Such knowledge is too wonderful for me, too great for me to understand! (Psalm 139:3–6)

3. Does God have the power to stop this, if he chose to?
   - You saw me before I was born. Every day of my life was recorded in your book. Every moment was laid out before a single day had passed. (Psalm 139:16–18)
   - I create the light and make the darkness. I send good times and bad times. I, the Lord, am the one who does these things. (Isaiah 45:7)

4. Do I believe God has a good plan for my life?
   - And we know that God causes everything to work together for the good of those who love God and are called according to his purpose for them. (Romans 8:28)
   - "For I know the plans I have for you," says the Lord. "They are plans for good and not for disaster, to give you a future and a hope." (Jeremiah 29:11)

If—and only if—you can honestly say yes to all four of these questions about your assurance of God's character, move on to the next three questions about your response to him.

5. What kind of attitude does God call me to?
   - Be thankful in all circumstances, for this is God's will for you who belong to Christ Jesus. (1 Thessalonians 5:18)
   - Always be full of joy in the Lord. I say it again—rejoice! . . . Don't worry about anything; instead, pray about everything. Tell God what you need, and thank him for all he has done. Then you will experience God's peace, which exceeds anything we can understand. (Philippians 4:4, 6–7)
   - Dear brothers and sisters, when troubles of any kind come your way, consider it an opportunity for great joy. (James 1:2)

6. How could I become more like Jesus through this experience?

- Teach me your ways, O LORD, that I may live according to your truth! Grant me purity of heart, so that I may honor you. (Psalm 86:11)
- I will teach you wisdom's ways and lead you in straight paths. (Proverbs 4:11)
- Put on your new nature, and be renewed as you learn to know your Creator and become like him. (Colossians 3:10)

7. Am I willing to obey him?
   - If you love me, obey my commandments. (John 14:15)
   - Don't you realize that you become the slave of whatever you choose to obey? You can be a slave to sin, which leads to death, or you can choose to obey God, which leads to righteous living. (Romans 6:16)
   - Trust in the LORD with all your heart; do not depend on your own understanding. Seek his will in all you do, and he will show you which path to take. (Proverbs 3:5–6)

> **PARENTING TIP**
> *When your children are having a hard time dealing with a difficult circumstance, go through these questions and verses with them.*

Trust is wonderfully freeing. It's what enables children to play and explore instead of worrying about dinner, to splash in a pool with their parents before they've learned to swim. I often think about Thanksgiving Day the year I was four, when I sat at the edge of a ten-foot balcony and dangled my feet over the patio below. My father came and stood below me and reached his hands in the air, smiling. "Jump into my arms," he said. I was momentarily stricken with fear. He wasn't tall enough to even touch my foot. "Jump into my arms," he said again. "I'll catch you."

Even at four years old, my understanding of gravity and concrete and bloody knees suggested that jumping from the balcony was a bad idea. But in that moment, I made a split decision to trust my dad over my own understanding, and my fear left me. If he said to jump, I knew it must be OK. And it was. More than fifty years later, I still remember the exhilaration of that fall into my father's arms. He smiled, and I knew he was pleased with me.

I'm not four anymore, and when my Father asks me to jump, the fall is a lot farther. And yet every time I've leaped at his call, his arms have eventually caught me. Every. Single. Time.

Personal Action

Earlier in this chapter, you were invited to make a commitment to defer to God's will. If you chose to write "Yes, Lord!" in your workbook, take the time now to write the same thing on an index card, then tape it somewhere you'll see it each day. This is a reminder of your pledge to say yes to whatever he has in store for you.

Rocket Prayer

"Lord, I choose to trust you to accomplish your plan for my life."

Say this prayer when you're worried about the future. Say it when your own plans fall through. Say it when you're honestly not sure God is there or if he has a good plan for you, and trust that even if you don't feel trusting deep in your bones, the Holy Spirit will help you get there.

Prayer of Response

Before you close this workbook for the rest of the week, take a few minutes to write a prayer of response to God. First, thank him for ways he has been good to you. Then, tell him what you're thinking and feeling as you process what you've learned.

Pass It On

This week, consider inviting your children into a trust exercise. Here are a couple of ideas:

- Ask your child to fall backward, trusting you'll catch him.
- Ask your child to swim to you in the pool, trusting you'll save her if she starts to sink.
- Ask your child to put a blindfold on and let you lead him around the house or even the neighborhood.

After the exercise is complete, take a few minutes to help your child process the experience. Did she feel anxious or afraid at the start? Why did she agree to your request? How does she feel now that she's safe? Explain that it's all the same with God. Sometimes he asks us to trust him, and that can feel scary. But he always has a plan, and he never lets us down.

If your child is old enough, consider having a deeper conversation about how he can trust God in a situation right now. Does he dislike a teacher at school? Have trouble with a particular kid in the neighborhood? Worry about not being as athletic as his peers? Teach him this week's rocket prayer, and lead him in a prayer asking for God to show him the path forward.

7

obedience: when God whispers

You are my friends
if you do what I command.

JOHN 15:14

When I was in my mid-forties, the Lord began seriously pestering me about my gossip habit. I'd brushed it off for a long time—after all, I wasn't malicious and I didn't spread people's deeply private information. I wasn't a classic gossip, always asking around about other people's business. Most of the time, I actually avoided situations where obvious gossip was taking place. But I wasn't always careful with my words and sometimes I went too far, venting my frustration about someone to a friend or laughing at someone's mishap, knowing that person would have been hurt if she'd been present.

I thought it wasn't a big deal, but the Lord disagreed. His whispers grew louder and louder. Finally, I let myself listen to his words, and conviction took hold. I confessed my sin and committed to taking responsibility for the habit. If I gossiped about someone, I'd told God, I would go to that person directly and apologize for my words.

Personal Reflection

Describe a moment in your life when you felt conviction in your conscience, but dismissed it. What argument did you use to convince yourself the behavior was OK?

Not long after making that commitment, I went to a tanning salon in our small town in preparation for a beach vacation. The woman behind the counter began talking about the halftime entertainment show at the high school basketball game the night before, during which the dance team had debuted a memorable routine. "I thought it was way too suggestive," she said, eyeing me for my opinion.

"Oh, yes. I noticed," I said, raising my eyebrows. I told her the woman next to me at the game had a lot of experience as a dancer. "She said she'd never seen anything as suggestive as this dance team," I told the clerk. "She said, 'It's more like pole dancing.'" At that moment, the door to a tanning stall opened and the captain of the dance team stepped out, glanced at us, put her head down, and quickly walked out the front door. She'd clearly heard everything.

Shame and conviction washed over me. I had just gossiped about a teenage girl I barely knew. And the next time I saw her, I was going to have to apologize to her.

Personal Reflection

Have you ever made a commitment to the Lord to handle a certain sin differently the next time it arose? If so, did you stick to that commitment? Explain.

When our conscience speaks, we get to decide to obey or disobey. Sometimes we make excuses, telling ourselves we're too busy or don't have the energy to deal with it at the moment. My excuse often sounds something like this: "Surely that wasn't really the Lord speaking. He couldn't really care about such minor details when there are so many huge injustices in this world." Silly me. He wants to refine our hearts and expel even the tiniest impurities so we can be in tune with him and walk with him. He is shaping each of us as a vessel for his Word and his work. When you feel your conscience twist, it's actually the Holy Spirit trying to pull that piece of dirt out of your golden soul. A spirit that allows this cleaning hears and understands the Lord better than one that holds on to sin, just like pure gold conducts electricity more effectively than gold tainted with contaminants.

In the last chapter, we talked about trust—trust that God will provide, that he has a good plan for our lives, that he will light our path if we seek his will. Obedience is the next natural step. It is always paired with trust. If we truly trust God has a good plan for our lives, then of course we will obey his directions. And if we're actively seeking his will, it would be foolish not to abide by it.

Oftentimes, our cultural misperception of obedience gets in the way. We see obedience as allowing someone else to tell us what to do—which, of course, our culture believes is a bad thing. We see it as submitting to constraints, as coloring inside the lines when our true selves want to decorate the whole page. But God's commands don't limit who we are. They help us be who we were created to be. I was not created to talk about God's other children behind their back, and that habit was preventing me from being my true created self. By teaching me to take responsibility for gossip, God was empowering me to flourish and be a positive influence in my community.

Personal Reflection

Take a minute to reflect on your own instinctive attitude about obedience and author-ity figures. Are you naturally quick to obey directions from others? Or do you despise being told what to do?

Think about where that attitude comes from. Is it a desire to be liked? A preference for being in control? A habit left over from childhood? Describe it.

How does your attitude about obedience to other people relate to your attitude about obedience to God?

About six months after the incident at the tanning salon, I ran into the dance team captain at a coffee shop, and we had a moment of awkward eye contact. I froze with dread, remembering my commitment to apologize to anyone I gossiped about. I did not want to embarrass myself in front of the friends I was meeting or humble myself in front of a bunch of her teenaged friends. I argued with myself that the Lord surely didn't want me to dredge up the ancient past, but I could almost picture God rolling his eyes.

I approached her. "Excuse me, Sarah," I said, "could I speak with you for a moment?" She looked terrified, but agreed. The result of my sin was obvious: she was hurt, afraid of my judgment, and there was an emotional wall between us. She knew I was a Christian, and that wall was a barrier that kept her from seeing Jesus in me.

"Sarah, do you remember that day in the tanning salon when I talked about the dance team?" I asked. She nodded. Her posture was rigid and her eyes were wide and nervous. "That was wrong of me," I said. "If I had talked to anyone, I should have talked to your dance coach. Will you please forgive me for what I said?" She looked briefly surprised, then visibly relaxed her posture and smiled. It was like her fear and anger melted. "Yes," she said, and I thanked her.

Putting aside my pride that day was really hard, but I'm so glad I did. Our God is passionate about redeeming relationships, and my willingness to embarrass myself blessed Sarah and created a relational connection that wasn't there before. More important, I know God was pleased in that moment, just as I am pleased when my own children obey me.

Personal Reflection

Describe a time when you gave your child instructions that were for his or her own good and your child disobeyed you.

How did you feel watching your child disobey?

As a mom, you know that not all obedience is equal. If you ask your child to make his bed and he does so halfway, hours later, or with a whiny attitude, your child isn't really fully obeying you. The same is true in our response to God. When we obey, we must aim to do so completely, immediately, and with a good attitude.

Let's start with what it looks like to obey **completely**. The principle is fairly clear. If you ask your son to empty the dishwasher and he only removes the plastic cups and plates, did he obey completely? Of course not. How about if he starts putting the silverware away, then gets distracted by attempting to organize the silverware drawer? Still no, even if he thinks he's being helpful.

As adults, we do this, too. For instance, you might skip polishing the grammar in a report at work, even if your boss asked you to deliver a finalized copy. If your oversight is pointed out, you play it off: "Oh, I just wanted to make sure you didn't want any big changes before I took care of that final step." Or, let's say you volunteer as the Sunday school teacher for kindergartners at church, and the children's coordinator instructs all the volunteers to lead their classes in five minutes of singing each Sunday, which you do not enjoy. You don't completely disregard the coordinator's instructions, but your singing time is unenthusiastic and you don't ask all the children to participate. Only a handful of kids stop playing and sing with you. Did you obey completely in either of these scenarios? No. You did enough to argue that you'd obeyed, but not enough to fully satisfy the intent of the instructions.

We do this all the time with the Lord. We feel a conviction to engage with our kids instead of trying to get them to leave us alone, so we compromise by silently watching television with them. We feel the Holy Spirit tug when we yell harshly at the dog, so we use a sweet, gentle tone to tell the mutt how dumb it is. The Lord is not fooled by this. His intention was for you to spend quality time building a trusting relationship with your kids and to treat your dog with kindness. A half-hearted response doesn't honor him or move you into the flourishing zone he wants for you.

Personal Reflection

Describe a time your child only partially obeyed your instructions. How did it affect you or others in your family?

Describe a recent or current way you're only partially obeying God.

Next up, **immediacy**: doing what you're told without delay. Let's use the dishwasher example again. You're fixing dinner and you ask your son to empty the dishwasher, and he yells "OK, mom!" from the next room. After dinner, the family goes to load their dirty dishes into the dishwasher and what do they find? Clean dishes. Even if your son fully intended to empty the dishwasher at some point that evening, his delay ruined the intention, which was that everyone would be able to load their own dishes into the dishwasher after the meal. In his mind he wasn't being disobedient, but his failure to respond when asked clearly isn't full obedience.

This, again, is something we do all the time as adults. For example, you might see a homeless man on a corner in your neighborhood and feel a prompting to provide a meal and clean water for him. But you've got groceries to unload and dinner to prepare, so you put it off. Later, after your own priorities are taken care of, you drive back to the corner with a sandwich and a water bottle—but he's gone. You could try to argue that you obeyed, but in reality, your failure to obey immediately means that neither you nor the man benefited as God intended.

God gives instructions when he does for a reason—just like you do with your kids. If he's prompting you to initiate a relationship with another mom at the YMCA, it might be because that mom really needs you right now. If he's bugging you about reading Scripture more consistently, it could be because he knows you need it to prepare for hardship coming this week. If we say we trust God's plan, we have to trust that his timing is good, too.

Personal Reflection

How does it make you feel when your children choose to continue playing or pursue their own priorities before obeying your instructions?

Describe a time when you've delayed responding to the Lord's whisper. (Maybe you're in the procrastinating phase now.)

The third and perhaps most crucial part of real obedience is obeying with a **good attitude**. Let's say your son stomps into the kitchen when you ask him to unload the dishwasher, whining and carelessly clanking the dishes together. He's so loud that he wakes up the baby, who is napping down the hall. If your intention was to have your son help you maintain peace and efficiency during meal prep and clean-up, then his behavior certainly doesn't fulfill your objective. More important, his behavior demonstrates heart rebellion. His hands might have technically obeyed your request, but he made it clear he had no desire to submit to you.

> **PARENTING TIP**
> *Remember that your children are watching you. The next time your boss calls you in for a late shift, be careful not to grumble about it. Choose to have a good attitude.*

I wouldn't consider this real obedience on my son's part, and I don't think God would consider it obedience if I behaved that way, either. And I do behave that way sometimes. We all do. We volunteer at church, but treat it like an annoying chore.

We donate money, but cringe at the effect on our bank account. We act on God's prompting to reach out to that new mom at school, but whine to our husband when she asks us to babysit her kids.

Attitude matters. It reflects your posture toward the Lord. And even if you're a pro at acting like you have a good attitude, remember that the Lord looks at the heart. His instructions are intended to bless you, bless others, and enable you to be who he created you to be. Miming the behavior with a grumpy heart does not honor him or reflect true trust in his will.

Personal Reflection

Describe a time when your child technically obeyed you, but did so with a nasty attitude. How did his or her actions affect your relationship in that moment?

Describe a time when you chose to obey God with a bad attitude. How did that affect your connection to God?

Obeying completely, immediately, and with a good attitude is really challenging. But here's the good news: in my experience, the Lord has often blessed me even in my half-hearted submission. For instance, I recall that time I prayed, "Thank you for allowing us to go through this" through gritted teeth after finding out about Blair's heart condition. At the Lord's prompting to give thanks in all circumstances, I did obey immediately and completely, but with a bitter, rebellious attitude. And you know what? He changed my heart, and within one minute I was offering genuine thanks. If you take a step toward the Lord, he will always meet you there and light up the next step on the path.

Think back to the story of Joseph in the previous chapter. Joseph didn't just have warm, fuzzy feelings about God despite immense hardship. He acted on his trust in the Lord by obeying his directions. He listened to God's guidance as it related to his work under Potiphar and the jailer. He told the cupbearer and Pharaoh what God had to say about their dreams—even though that might have felt risky and embarrassing. In the moment, we rarely know how our little choice to obey will further God's kingdom on earth. We don't know how it will lead to goodness later in our story. But the Lord said, "trust in the LORD with all your heart," and there is no trust without obedience.

Note: If you find yourself stuck, seemingly unable to fully obey, revisit those seven questions from the previous chapter. Trust and obedience always go together, and those questions are just as relevant here.

Personal Action

Identify one area in your life where you are not fully obeying the Lord's instructions.

Write down what needs to be done to take full and quick action. Then, actually take those action steps this week.

Rocket Prayer

"Lord, give me the courage and desire to obey you."

Obedience takes courage—especially when the request involves swallowing your pride. Say this prayer when you feel your conscience twist. The Lord may be the one asking something of you, but he's also the one who will help you do it.

Prayer of Response

Before you close this workbook for the rest of the week, take a few minutes to write a prayer of response to God. First, thank him for ways he has been good to you. Then, tell him what you're thinking and feeling as you process what you've learned.

Pass It On

Consider sharing what you've learned with your kids this week by using a game to demonstrate obedience and disobedience. While you're playing with your child, say, "Let's play a game. You're going to be the mommy [or daddy], and I'm going to be the kid. You get to tell me what to do." Your child will probably jump at this. At first, obey your child. If she says to roll on the ground, roll on the ground. But after a while, start disobeying. Trust me: it won't take long for her to get irritated and impatient. When she does, calmly sit down and ask, "How did it feel when I disobeyed you?" She'll probably say it felt bad. Explain that you feel bad too when she disobeys you. Remind her that you're the mommy in real life, and that when you ask her to do something, it isn't a game. You're asking for a reason.

Also, if you have kids who are old enough, consider looking for an opportunity to loop back around to an instance of disobedience earlier in the day. Whether you're in the car or going through a bedtime routine, ask your child if he remembers ignoring your directions (or complying with a bad attitude). Ask him why he behaved that way, and respond to his answer with a balance of grace and firm coaching. For instance, you might say, "I understand that you would have preferred to continue playing outside. I love being outside, too. But when you cleared the table with a bad attitude, you were making it clear that what I want isn't as important as what you want. I don't boss you around for no reason. That's not my job. My job is to help you grow up to be an adult that is responsible and kind and loves Jesus. Next time, I need you to respect me by obeying with a good attitude."

8

surrender: grapes and marbles

Submit to God, and you will have peace;
then things will go well for you.

JOB 22:21

When I was fifteen years old, I took a job at a Christian summer camp where teenage employees handled basic janitorial and maintenance work. Workers rotated every two weeks doing jobs like setting tables, washing dishes, serving food, and doing laundry for the staff. Running the candy store was the best job in the camp and bathroom cleaning, called "biffy duty," was the worst job—so bad that leadership gave afternoons off to the crew handling bathroom duty.

My crew boss made it clear from day one she did not like me, so I wasn't surprised when I was assigned to biffy duty for the first rotation. *Oh well,* I thought, *at least I'll get it over with early in the summer.* One day during the second week I got really sick. I managed to finish my cleaning duties, but afterward I left a message for my boss, Jamie, to let her know I wouldn't be at Bible study and dinner. I went to my cabin, curled up, and went to sleep. Within an hour Jamie burst into the room, slamming the door so hard I remember thinking the window might crack. Her face was red and furrowed and she screamed at me, "Get up and start packing! You are going home!" She left without another word.

Sick and confused, I was summoned to the camp director's office, where I explained what happened. He listened quietly, then laid out a challenge I will never forget. "You have done nothing to deserve being sent home," he told me. "Therefore, you have a choice to make. You can stay or go home—but if you choose to stay, you must do what Jamie says with a good attitude. You have to surrender your rights. If you do not want to do that, you can let her win and go home." I was upset and a little scared by what had happened, but I also knew that God understood what was going on and was on my side. So, I chose to stay.

Needless to say, it was a tough summer. While the rest of the crew rotated through various jobs, I got assigned to biffy duty every single week. Jamie gleefully filled my afternoons with extra jobs, even though the other bathroom cleaners had the afternoons off. She bullied me every chance she got, and some of my peers followed her lead, teasing me or, at the least, ignoring me.

Personal Reflection

Do you have a memory of being bullied by a peer or treated unfairly by a parent, teacher, coach, family member, or other figure? Describe it.

How did you respond in that situation?

I was determined not to disappoint the camp director or the Lord, even though Jamie's actions hurt, confused, and angered me. As someone who hates to be controlled by others, submitting to Jamie took everything I had. In fact, it took more—it took the Lord. I am naturally prone to fighting back, and I wanted to put an end to her injustice. Yet the Lord made it clear to me that he would be the one to enact justice—that my job was to surrender and persevere. I frequently retreated to my cabin, where a girl had taped the following quote above her bed. (The first two lines come from Richard Lovelace's poem "To Althea, from Prison.")

Stone walls do not a prison make,
Nor iron bars a cage:
Your true liberty lies within your soul
And not in the circumstances
You may find yourself in.

That summer, my liberty lay in the Lord—not in fighting back or escaping Jamie's mistreatment. With eyes on him, I plowed through somehow. The Lord did not remove me from this situation. Instead, he allowed me to remain in an unjust and unhealthy dynamic for over two months. Yet I would not trade that summer. It is one of the most profound lessons of my life, and it set me on a path of beautiful surrender to the Lord.

Twenty-five years later I saw a woman who had been a camp counselor that year. Out of the blue, she said, "Remember that summer at camp when you cleaned biffies all summer?" I told her I couldn't possibly forget. "I was amazed at the positive attitude you always had," she said. At that moment, I thanked the Lord. He was confirming for me that not only had he been working in my life, but that my actions positively affected those around me—so much that a counselor remembered my surrender a quarter of a century later.

Personal Reflection

How does the idea of submitting to unjust or difficult circumstances sit with you? What emotions does that stir up?

Reflect on whether that attitude is shaped more by culture or Scripture. Think about Jesus's example.

Surrender is an extension of obedience. It is a posture of yielding to the Lord, a recognition that God sits on the throne all the time, not just when you choose to put him there. Being obedient means complying fully when the Lord gives you instructions. Living a life of surrender takes that one step further, requiring you to actually seek out God's instructions in daily life—and then, of course, obey them.

Surrender is especially challenging in the moments we face biffy duty—when a boss, family member, friend, or authority figure criticizes us, limits us, or treats us unfairly. Most of us immediately experience a rush of adrenaline pumping through our veins. Our fists clench and we instinctively react with anger, defensiveness, or passive aggression. But we always have a choice, and it comes down to this: are you going to respond like a marble or like a grape?

A marble, of course, is a ball of glass. It is hard and inflexible. When you apply pressure with a hard object, like a hammer, the marble often roles out from underneath. This is how most of us respond to life. We refuse to give in, and we resist or remove ourselves from tough situations, trying to dodge pressure the Lord is allowing in our life. But one swift direct hit with a hammer and a marble shatters into dangerous little pieces of glass. In the same way, when we resist what the Lord allows into our life, we eventually crack and shatter—and the shards wound us and those around us.

A grape, on the other hand, is a soft, malleable, living thing. It is flexible and vulnerable. When you apply pressure, the grape surrenders—easily squishing beneath the hammer. There's no need to whack it. And where there was a grape before, the pressure leaves behind something far more valuable: wine. This is the response God calls us to. When we respond as grapes, we do not run from God's teaching moments. We keep our eyes on him and give way to his teaching, allowing him to squish whatever he wants. He makes wine every time.

Just like we might use a hammer, God uses people and situations as tools. In my life that summer, he used Jamie. My surrender was not about empowering or affirming her, and it didn't signify that what she did was OK. It was not. My surrender was about allowing God to use Jamie as a tool to make me more like his Son. With Jamie, God crushed my pride, my entitlement, and my self-sufficiency. With those gone, the good that seeped out—trust, perseverance, dependence—has aged with me, getting better and better with time.

Personal Reflection

Describe a season in your life story when God squished you and you saw something beautiful come out of it.

Now, I've mentored women long enough to know that some of you are deeply uncomfortable right now. The idea of surrendering to injustice makes your skin crawl, even if you can wrap your brain around the principle of responding like a grape. Before you write this idea off entirely, let's look at a practical example of surrender.

Let's say that, one evening, you're helping the kids with a school craft when your husband gets home from work. Before kissing you or asking about your day, he asks whether you have anything cooking for dinner—and his tone comes across as surprisingly critical. You tell him that no, nothing is cooking. You've been swamped with the kid's homework, and you were thinking that take-out might be the best option tonight. He immediately snaps at you, asking what you could possibly have been doing all day. The house is a wreck and you haven't prepared any food and it's too expensive to get take-out all the time. He accuses you of being lazy and demands that you make a meal at home—*now*.

In this moment, you have a choice. You can react in your own way—whether that's snapping back, acting passive-aggressive all evening, or silently resenting him for the mistreatment—or, as an act of surrender to God, you can pray and ask the Lord how he wants you to respond.

Let's say you choose surrender. Instead of responding to your husband immediately, you let silence hang in the air for a few seconds. In your head, you pray: "Lord, how do you want me to respond?" A gut feeling sinks in and tells you that, this time, you need to graciously yield instead of fighting back or calling your husband out on his rudeness. Something tells you there's more to the story than you're aware of, and that the Lord will be the one to seek change and justice. So, you respond aloud with warmth. "Sure," you say. "I'll get started on a quick meal right now. Would you mind helping the kids clean off the table?" Disarmed by your kindness, he agrees and the evening proceeds without incident.

Over the next two months, your husband continues to snap at you for small things, and the Lord continues to ask that you let it slide. But one thing does begin to change: you. As much as you hate admitting it, you begin to see that your husband might have been right—you do tend to be a little lazy when it comes to meals. You don't enjoy cooking, and you prefer to use busyness as an excuse to go to a restaurant or order delivery, which is an expensive habit that strains your bank account. So, you decide to prioritize saving money on food by meal-planning at the start of each week and preparing almost all lunches and dinners at home.

Your husband no longer has a reason to snap at you about meals, so the offenses diminish. He does still bark at you sometimes, though, especially when he feels like you are correcting or criticizing him. As usual, you go to God before responding. And, as usual, he continues to ask you to yield. Through continued prayer, the Lord reveals to you that you do have a pattern of being critical—of your friends, your kids, your husband—and he helps you work on taming that critical voice. Everyone seems to respond to this change, acting more relaxed and comfortable around you than they did before. As the months pass, your husband slowly softens and gains better control of his temper.

Now, let's look back at what happened in that story. There are three key takeaways that are important for understanding surrender.

First, your submission was ultimately to the Lord (who is always good), not to your husband (who was being a jerk). This is true every time you respond as a grape. At camp, it might have looked to others like I was submitting to Jamie. But really, I was submitting to God, who kept telling me surrender was the right choice.

> **PARENTING TIP**
> *When you choose to surrender graciously in tense situations at home, you are subtly teaching your children to respond with surrender, too.*

Second, your gracious responses denied your husband any justification for his unkindness. If you had snapped back at him or treated him with contempt, he might have used it as an excuse, telling himself you're ungrateful for how hard he works or you're always pointing out the worst in him.

Third, the Lord used a bad situation to produce something truly good. He took your husband's unkindness and, through your surrender, turned it into greater peace and financial stability in your family. You could have developed a pattern of bickering with your husband. Instead, you developed more self-awareness and adopted healthy habits that benefit your family.

In this story, there isn't a clear moment of reconciliation. Your husband did not come to you and apologize, nor did the Lord prompt you to initiate a conversation about his attitude. Sometimes that's how it goes. But it isn't always the case. Sometimes, instead of asking you to yield, the Lord will prompt you to action. And when he does, he'll give you wisdom so you can be effective. Sometimes, the Lord will convict the other person and they will confess and apologize to you. The outcome isn't really what matters. What matters is that God is the one in control.

So, do you see? Surrender is not about rolling over in front of the bad guys. It's about deciding that God's will should be done, not your own. It's about letting him work in your own heart instead of trying to change others. This is why responding like a grape does not go against the Christian value of seeking justice. The Lord may very well call you to action—whether that means defending someone who is being bullied, advocating for equality, or simply initiating a conversation with your spouse.

Let me throw out this caveat: If you are in a situation where you're in physical danger, get out. Get to safety, praying as you go for guidance and protection. You can make space later to ask God what he'd like you to do next, and he will show you. If you're in the middle of an ongoing situation that raises a red flag for you, please talk to your mentor.

Personal Action

Take a moment to pray, right now, that the Lord will help you turn to him first the next time you're exposed to mistreatment. Make a commitment that you will turn to him rather than reacting or responding to the situation. Use an "I will" statement to make this commitment.

Most of us don't run into a Jamie every day. Our seasons of pressure from the hammer, whether time spent under a miserable boss or a conflict with administrators at our child's school, are often punctuated by seasons of ordinariness. These seasons are the perfect time to practice surrender in the small things. How can you hope to respond like a grape in defining moments of crisis if you're not in the habit of surrendering when your children snap at you? God provides opportunities to choose to be a marble or a grape every day.

I have a clear memory of an afternoon at home when my son Cavan was about sixteen. Three of his friends were hanging out, laughing, and snacking with him in the kitchen. My friend, Patricia, had come over to visit with me, and as we headed into the family room she rudely blurted, "Cavan, bring me a glass of water."

My hackles went up at Patricia's tone. How dare she speak to my son that way! We were just a few feet from the kitchen. She could have easily gotten water for herself or asked me, politely, for a glass. But I didn't say anything. Cavan had always been clever, and I wanted to see how he would respond.

Personal Reflection

Name a moment recently when someone was rude to you or inadvertently irritated you.

How did you respond?

Unsurprisingly, the laughter in the kitchen awkwardly halted as the teens looked from Patricia to Cavan to me. My son paused, looked at Patricia, smiled sweetly, and said, simply, "OK." He graciously excused himself from his friends, poured her a glass of water, and brought it to her with a polite smile. I searched his face for anger or sarcasm and saw none. At that moment, I felt both shame and pride—shame that I responded inside like a marble and immense pride that my son had responded like such a gracious grape. His willingness to be squished immediately dissipated the awkwardness in the room and modeled surrender to his peers—and to Patricia and me.

Personal Action

Name three areas where you consistently respond like a marble, and make a plan to respond as a grape this week instead. For instance, maybe you fight back or leave the room when your mother-in-law provides unwanted feedback on your household skills. What would it look like for you to stay in the room and submit to her?

Rocket Prayer

"Lord, help me surrender to your will."

Say this prayer when your plans get interrupted. Say this prayer when your coworker or your mother-in-law steps on your toes. Say this prayer when your kids leave you feeling completely out of control.

Responding like a grape is hard—even in little daily challenges. I promise, even the best over-achiever can't magically turn into a grape out of sheer willpower. We must call on the Lord again and again for help.

Prayer of Response

Before you close this workbook for the rest of the week, take a few minutes to write a prayer of response to God. First, thank him for ways he has been good to you. Then, tell him what you're thinking and feeling as you process what you've learned.

Pass It On

Read the story of Jesus's betrayal, trial, torture, and crucifixion with your kids. Ask them if Jesus did anything to deserve that kind of treatment. No? Ask them if that means it was unfair. Yes? Ask what they do when they think they are being treated unfairly. Finally, ask them how Jesus responded in the story when he was treated unfairly. Have a conversation about how Jesus's willingness to surrender to unfairness led to the greatest good in all of history. Talk about what it might look like for them to surrender next time they want to get mad.

You can also teach your kids the grape-or-marble concept with a hands-on activity. After school, grab a grape, a marble, and a hammer. Do a little experiment showing how the marble tries to escape pressure and the grape squishes. Let them lick up the grape juice. Talk about how the marble would break if you hit it hard enough. Ask your child which is better: shards of glass or grape juice? Tell your child that life is like the hammer—it hits us sometimes, and we have to decide whether to respond like a grape or a marble. That is, we have a choice whether to make glass shards or grape juice. Teach them this week's rocket prayer, and tell them you're always there to help them figure out how to respond to hard situations, such as when other kids are mean.

DEALING WITH THE PAST

THREE WEEKS

In this section, we will explore our life stories and work through our bitterness toward God, others, and ourselves, creating space for freedom and deep relationship.

9

knowing your story

You made all the delicate, inner parts of my body
and knit me together in my mother's womb. . . .
Every day of my life was recorded in your book.
Every moment was laid out
before a single day had passed.

PSALM 139:13,16

My friend Lisa is energetic and bubbly, so I immediately knew something was wrong the day she came into my office looking concerned. She shared that she and her fifth-grade daughter, Andrea, had been arguing a lot lately. They just didn't seem to connect. When I asked for an example, she said, "Andrea had set out her favorite red dress to wear on the first day of school yesterday, and when I saw it I just told her, 'You are not allowed to wear dresses to school!' She argued with me and hasn't really talked to me since. It continues to affect our relationship and the way she treats her little brother."

Lisa looked at me, expecting me to take her side and agree that Andrea had an attitude problem. But something else stood out to me. She had spit out the rule—"You are not allowed to wear dresses to school!"—with such harshness. I asked why she didn't want Andrea to wear a dress. She wrinkled her brow and thought and then said, "I guess it's because I don't want her to be teased." Hmm. I asked why she thought her daughter would get teased if she wore a dress to school. Lisa looked at her hands for a while and finally said, "I was teased in grade school for having dirty and unstylish clothes. One day on the playground I wore a special dress and a boy saw my underwear as I climbed the ladder to go down the slide. He teased me for a long time."

The pain of that experience was clear on her face. It had been at least twenty years since that day on the playground, but the memory still made her uncomfortable—and, without her knowledge at the time, it had influenced a parenting decision and hurt her child's sensitive heart.

We all live in the context of story. We were born in circumstances out of our control. Our parents, siblings, community, race, socioeconomic status, and local culture all shaped our lives and our lenses from day one. We had moments that taught us what joy was. We had moments that instilled fear. We had moments that left heart bruises. We made decisions—and had decisions made for us—that set us up for heartache or failure later. We were betrayed. We were embarrassed. We were proud. We were admired. And, like Lisa, we are unknowingly influenced by all of those things.

As you move toward Foundational Parenting, it's essential that you reflect on your story, because self-awareness is essential to Foundational Living. You might be instilling in your children the same fears you learned at their age. You might be unleashing rage at them because you haven't dealt with long-ignored hurts. You might be pushing them toward the goals that felt fulfilling for you, even if they aren't helpful for your child's temperament.

PARENTING TIP

Question yourself when you react strongly to something small. Could something from your past be subconsciously at play?

We will be dedicating this entire chapter to crafting a timeline of your memories and exploring the patterns in your life. I know it's a lot to ask. Alongside your joyful memories there are inevitably painful ones. You might have been hurt badly enough that you've spent years trying to forget—and the last thing you want to do is write those memories down or discuss them with a mentor. After all, you're trying to move forward. To become a better mom. Revisiting the past might seem counterintuitive, but I believe this will ultimately be a healing exercise for you—even if it feels painful at first. Did you know studies show that verbalizing your story actually leads to physical healing in the brain? I think it's amazing that God hardwired us with a pathway to healing, and that the path, just like the Christian life, requires truth and community.

Let me preface this exercise with a plea: if you have experienced serious trauma in your life that you haven't dealt with, please see a Christian counselor. This workbook is not an in-depth trauma-healing tool. Depending on the severity, you may need to prioritize seeing a professional for a couple of months before continuing with this workbook. The rest of this chapter is not worth your time if you are unwilling to honestly face significant hurts in your past. Time does not heal all wounds. For your sake and that of your children, seek help. It's time.

Personal Action

First, intentionally set aside a couple of hours to focus on your timeline. You can do this all at once or spread it over a few days. Whatever works for you. Just don't put it off until the night before you meet with your mentor. Believe me—this can be time consuming and emotional.

To begin, break down your life into manageable chunks of time. It's too hard to think about all of your life at once. You can do this by focusing on five or ten years at a time or by focusing on phases of life, such as life before you started kindergarten, life during middle school, and life between graduating from college and getting married. Most of us think about our lives in terms of phases, so this might be the most natural option.

Moving through these chunks in chronological order, record any and all memories—mundane, frightening, joyful, embarrassing, whatever. If you have painful memories in your story that you aren't ready to describe in words, simply use an abbreviation or a code word. As you progress to adult years when you likely have many clear and insignificant memories, it's OK to stop writing every single memory you can recall. Record the ones that stir emotion of any kind, even if it wasn't ultimately a significant moment.

Finish this timeline before moving on to the next chapter—even if it takes you more than a week. Write the due date for finishing the timeline here: _____.

I was in my forties when I first mapped a timeline of my life. I remember being surprised by how much my past formed who I had become. Think back to that distinct early morning memory where I learned the thrill of trusting when I jumped into my dad's arms from a second-story balcony. And another was the sweet comfort of my mom's voice calling up to me from the bottom of the stairs at night, telling me everything was all right and I didn't need to panic when I woke up in the dark or couldn't go to sleep. Another was the hurt of being teased about my weight and rejected by friends for choosing not to drink in high school. All these and more formed my character and influenced the way I respond to the people and situations I encounter every day.

Whatever you are feeling in the aftermath of writing a timeline, know that it's normal. It's healthy to feel. Know that the Lord cares and longs for you to share those feelings with him, even if they are feelings of hurt, anger, or bitterness. Know that the Lord is heartbroken by the ways that brokenness in this world has hurt you. Know that no matter what bad decisions you've made, his hand is always extended in invitation to you. He invites you, every day, to enter into *his* story.

One of the best things about writing a timeline is that it empowers you to see patterns. Looking back through my own key memories, I saw a trend: I had a prideful, independent spirit. I liked being in control and I resisted being controlled or dependent on others. Yet I also saw that the Lord repeatedly wove moments into my story that taught me to surrender control—the very thing I needed to learn most.

Personal Reflection

Looking back at your life, what patterns do you see? Have you consistently strived to be liked or needed by other people? Strived for success, independence, or control? Security or comfort? Perfection or uniqueness?

Pick one or two patterns that resonate most deeply, and consider the following questions: How have those patterns influenced your relationship with God?

How have those patterns influenced your relationships with others, such as your friends, parents, spouse, boss, or faith community?

How have those patterns affected your identity as a parent?

How have you pushed those patterns onto your kids?

If your mentor has known you for a long time, ask her if she sees those patterns—and what others you might be missing. If your mentor is a relatively new person in your life, consider asking a longtime friend or family member to speak into this.

We all have consistent patterns in our lives, and the reality is that they are part of our story and will probably always have an effect on us. I still try to take control, and I have to remind myself that I can trust God to handle things. Being aware of that tendency has empowered me to catch myself and pay attention to God's invitations to vulnerability and healthy dependence.

Whatever your story, whatever your life patterns, know this: God sees you and knows you and loves you. You are forgiven and whole.

Personal Action

Summon your bravery and vulnerability and review your timeline with your mentor. Remember that verbalizing your story leads to healing. Your mentor will share her story with you, too.

Rocket Prayer

"Lord, help me see things as you see them."

We all see the world through our own unique lens—and those lenses are inherently tainted by our life experiences. They're not the same lens through which God sees. By asking God to help us see through his lens, we're ultimately asking him to rescue us from being controlled by our past.

Say this prayer when you feel emotion rise up and you don't know why. Say this prayer when a voice in your head tells you you're not good enough. Say this prayer every single morning when you get out of bed. It's essential to know your story. It's not necessary to be controlled by it.

Prayer of Response

Before you close this workbook for the rest of the week, take a few minutes to write a prayer of response to God. First, thank him for ways he has been good to you. Then, tell him what you're thinking and feeling as you process what you've learned.

Pass It On

This week, tell your kids about one of the major life patterns you identified earlier in this chapter. Your children love you and want to know you, and it's healthy for them to see you as human—especially as they get older. Confessing your shortcomings to your children makes it safer for them to do the same with you. For instance, if you have a tendency to demand perfection from your kids because you also demand it of yourself, look for an opportunity to confess this to them. You might say, "This week I realized that I have a tendency to be too hard on you. I sometimes get mad or frustrated when you don't do things perfectly. The truth is that I've always expected myself to be perfect, and I am really hard on myself. Without meaning to, I've extended that expectation to you, too. I am sorry for that. Will you forgive me?" Talk to your mentor about how your kids responded to this.

Also, help your kids make a timeline of their own life as a craft. Invite them to draw pictures of their memories, both happy and sad, and use a binder or stapler to turn the collection into a memory book. With each new picture, take the opportunity to have a conversation with your child about that memory. How did that memory make them feel and why? What did they learn from this memory?

10

repentance: turning back on the road

If we confess our sins to him, he is faithful and just to forgive us our sins and to cleanse us from all wickedness.

1 JOHN 1:9

One afternoon when my husband, Don, was about ten years old, he and his best friend paid a visit to the neighbor's house because they knew there was always a bowl of candy on the coffee table. No one answered the doorbell. But the boys—who were really craving a treat—were not dissuaded. They decided to sneak in through a side door.

Just as the boys reached for the side door's knob, the door swung open—and there was Mac, the homeowner, who had just woken up because he worked a night shift. He asked what the boys wanted, and Don quickly said, "We knocked on the front door and thought somebody said 'come in.'" After a brief interrogation, the boys left and went home—each hoping Mac would be too sleepy to remember.

Later, Don's mom confronted him about the incident. Mac's wife had come over and told her the boys tried to break in. Though he knew it was wrong, Don stuck to his lie. "No, we thought someone said to 'come in.'" His mother pushed, but Don was resolute. "We weren't trying to break in," he insisted. "God knows the truth even if you won't believe me!"

Personal Reflection

Describe a time—years ago or recently—when you ignored your conscience. What feelings did you have and why?

Don had long since forgotten about that childhood sin until our children were young, and he was really growing in his faith. The Lord had been challenging him to take down his walls and engage in an unhindered way. So, when the Holy Spirit brought this memory to mind and challenged Don to confess his sin to Mac, he knew it was a test. Would he drive three hours to humiliate himself in front of an old neighbor, or would he ignore the Lord's command and, in doing so, put up a barrier between himself and God?

Don chose to listen to his conscience and humble himself. Not only that, but he took our youngest daughter with him for the long Saturday excursion so that she could learn by watching her father repent. When Don arrived at Mac's home, he confessed the truth about that day and asked for Mac's forgiveness. Mac—who was by that time a very elderly man with a terminal illness—remembered the incident and immediately forgave Don, and they ended up having a very sweet visit.

Personal Reflection

Describe a time you owned up and asked for forgiveness after losing your temper, telling a lie, or otherwise wronging someone else. How did you feel before you confessed? How did you feel afterward?

How did that conversation influence the relationship?

If you can't think of an example, consider why. Do you push things under the rug, hoping they'll go away? Do you have a hard time admitting you're wrong?

I love this story about Don because it's such a great example of true repentance.

Many of us think of repentance simply as regret or saying sorry, but God's perspective on repentance is far more profound. Repentance is not simply the feeling of regret or saying the words, "I'm sorry." At its core, repentance is the process of turning away from sin and moving toward God so he can remove shame and provide healing.

To understand repentance more deeply, we have to talk about sin. Sin is anything you embrace—internally or externally—that draws you away from the Lord. I picture it this way: As you are walking down the path of your life, each choice is a fork in the road. Either you go to the right toward the Lord, or to the left toward selfish desires. The left is alluring. It promises the things we crave most, such as comfort, happiness, security, or approval. The right is challenging, and often we can't see where the path leads. We all face these choices, and we either go left or right. When we go left, we sin.

It's worth noting that according to this definition, sin is not necessarily a classically bad behavior, which is how we often think about it. It could be a seemingly neutral behavior, such as a purchase or a decision about whether to attend an event, that ignored what God was prompting you to do in that situation. It's not about whether your actions are "good" or "bad"—it's about whether you chose to move toward the Lord or toward your selfish nature.

When we take the path to the left, we inherently turn our backs on God, who is patiently waiting in the other direction. Not only that, but our sins create big rocks between us and the godly path. These boulders make it harder to see and hear God and harder to get back on the right path, especially as they accumulate. (For instance, when Don lied to his mom, he made it even harder to confess and come clean.) Sometimes after a decision to sin we keep going, maybe without even looking back. But sometimes we recognize our selfish choice, turn around, navigate over or around the boulders, and find the correct path. This is repentance. The amazing thing is that the Lord doesn't wait for us in a fixed place back on his side of the path, leaving us to figure out how to reach him. He meets us right where we are the second we turn around, and he helps us navigate through the mess we've created.

Personal Reflection

Take a minute to pray. Ask God to show you the left turns you've made that you haven't dealt with yet.

Put a checkmark by the hardest one.

In practice, repentance breaks down into five steps:

1. **Recognize:** Acknowledge that you have sinned and that you need forgiveness from the Lord.
2. **Receive:** Accept the Lord's forgiveness and peace.
3. **Resolve:** Make a decision to change your future behavior and put safeguards in place to help you make the right choice next time.
4. **Release:** Bring the sin into the light by confessing and asking forgiveness of the person (or people) you wronged.
5. **Reconcile:** Take responsibility for the damage caused by your sin and make it right, if possible.

When God challenged Don to repent for his childhood lie, he didn't simply ask Don to apologize and ask forgiveness through prayer. He also asked Don to confess the sin to Mac, too. In doing so, Don brought his sin out of hiding and into the light. He also affirmed Mac as having been right all those years ago, which helped make right the emotional damage he'd caused.

Now, in Don's case, the Holy Spirit's prompting felt clear and unavoidable. But for most of us, hearing from the Holy Spirit is a mysterious concept. We know he lives in us and speaks to us, but we often don't know what we're listening for. Here's a tip: when it comes to sin, a word from the Holy Spirit feels just like what you might describe as a tug on your conscience. You know the feeling. It's that instant regret and internal wince that comes after you snap at your children or gossip about a friend.

Here's the thing: our enemy uses that feeling to produce shame, which makes us want to hide our sin from others and from the Lord. When the Enemy succeeds in that moment, we tell our conscience to hush and hope no one noticed our sin. But God intends that feeling to produce remorse and call us to repentance. He loves us dearly, and he knows that repentance is what's best for us—what will help us thrive. Without it, we're stuck on a bad path and we have trouble connecting with him. It's right there in that moment of instant regret that he invites us to begin the process of the five R's, because he doesn't want us to spend any more time disconnected from him than we have to.

Personal Reflection

Consider the sin you checkmarked a few minutes ago. How did that left turn hurt other people?

If you have trouble identifying who might have been hurt and how, I encourage you to dig deep. Few—if any—sins are truly just between you and God. For example, let's say you chose to buy yourself an expensive purse, even though you felt a twinge in your conscience. Consider how that financial choice affects your family. Did you wrong your spouse by spending shared money in an irresponsible way? Will your children feel the loss (even if they don't know it) by not getting to experience something enriching that the money could have provided?

There are a lot of reasons we choose not to repent. Sometimes, we don't even consider it because we aren't willing to put God above our selfish desires. Sometimes we are afraid of what repentance might require us to do. Sometimes, we're deaf to God's call and don't realize we've sinned. Other times, we hear God's call and perhaps desire to repent, but Satan gets in the way. Let's examine a few of our enemy's favorite lines and see if they hold up.

"Confession will cause you more shame than you already have." When we have done something wrong, shame is our conscience trying to move us to the action of repentance. This action is humbling at first, but confessing removes shame and produces freedom and peace.

"You won't have consequences if you hide it." Not true. Sin is like a cancer in your life. Concealing a sin is like refusing an operation to remove a tumor or infection, and therefore hiding a sin has serious personal consequences. Not only that, but you usually have to deceive others in order to keep the sin secret, and this causes relational distance. The consequences of hiding a sin might seem farther off or more vague than the consequences of repentance, but they will come and they will hurt.

> **PARENTING TIP**
> *Don't ask your kids to say a quick, empty "I'm sorry" to their friends or siblings. Use questions to guide your child to genuine repentance.*

"Just quickly say sorry and move on. That is enough." Our enemy loves shortcuts. Just saying the words "I'm sorry"—especially if it's only after you got caught—isn't the same as turning back on the road. If there's no heartfelt remorse, no real recognition of your wrong, and no efforts to take steps toward reconciliation, it's just empty words. (You know exactly what this looks like, because you've done it and you've seen your children do it.)

"You're a bad person and deserve to wallow in your shame." Jesus doesn't want you to stay trapped in the sludge. He says, "Come to me all who are weary and burdened and I will give you rest." When you choose to repent, he removes the shame. We are not meant to live with shame.

Personal Reflection

Consider the sin you named a few minutes ago. What's kept you from repenting?

Spend a few minutes journaling about that as a written prayer to God. Be honest with him about what's holding you back—he already knows the truth anyway.

Back in 2007, I had the opportunity to speak in Uganda at a women's conference on repentance and forgiveness, and it was on that journey that I witnessed one of the most remarkable examples of repentance I've ever seen.

After one of the sessions, I asked the women to break up into small groups and pray. The focus of their small group time was to repent for holding grudges so they would be able to forgive those who had hurt them. During this prayer time, my interpreter, Claudia, approached me excitedly and told me that three women from an enemy tribe were in attendance, and they wanted to apologize for what their tribe had done to Claudia's people over the years.

What had the enemy tribe done? They had raided the other tribe's villages, raped their women, killed their men, and stole their livelihoods. This was an enormous decision. I'd heard the stories, and I knew the Lord was working a miracle right there in our meeting. I said to Claudia, "That is amazing, Praise God! Why don't you go over and pray with them while we are finishing up, and then we will have them talk to the whole group?"

Claudia's face immediately fell from excitement to fear. I asked what was wrong. "You don't know what they have done," she said. "Last year, members of their tribe murdered my cousin. They stabbed him in the back and shot him in the head—and then took pictures of his bloody body and sent them to his wife. I have been angry and bitter at them ever since."

These people were not just a theoretical enemy tribe. They were truly Claudia's enemies. They had hurt her family in a gruesome way and made life hard and frightening for her people. Any one of us would feel angry and bitter, and many of us would argue Claudia had every right to hold on to that anger and bitterness. But here's the thing: Jesus says clearly that unforgiveness is sin, even when it seems entirely justified. He calls us to extend forgiveness in the same way that God extends forgiveness to us.

In that moment at the conference, Claudia had a choice. She had been harboring unforgiveness toward her enemies, and she could either continue to do so, or she could repent of that sin and seek reconciliation with the women from the enemy tribe.

I took a deep breath. "Claudia," I said, "God wants you to repent of your anger and bitterness." She paused, then looked into my eyes and softly said, "OK." She immediately dropped to her knees, put her face to the ground, and began sobbing. For a few minutes, she cried and prayed aloud in her native language. I watched in amazement at her willingness to repent. When she was done, she stood up, wiped her face, and boldly said, "OK, I'm ready." With that, she turned and walked over to the corner where the women from the other tribe were watching and waiting. All the anger and bitterness had gone from her. She took their hands and began singing and praying with them, and her actions had a far-reaching effect that day—something I'll tell you more about in the next chapter.

You see, next week we're going to talk about forgiveness. Repentance and forgiveness are closely intertwined. As you can see in this story, extending forgiveness to someone else almost always means repenting of the unforgiveness you were harboring before. Even if we were not responsible for the conflict, we are responsible for our attitudes and actions before, during, and after it. Horrific events like this often take time to process, but we must repent of our own bitterness in order to be free.

Personal Reflection

Revisit your left turn list above and your timeline from the last chapter. What hurts in your past do you still feel bitter about? Who do you hold anger and bitterness toward?

Take a few minutes to journal about that as a written prayer to God. If you don't feel ready to repent, pray and ask the Lord to soften your heart first, then move ahead.

There is something transformative about repentance. It softens our hearts, and allows us to see and hear God better. It removes shame and provides peace and healing. Like we see in the stories about Don and Claudia, repentance removes barriers between us and the Lord—and between us and others.

Personal Action

Consider the sins you named earlier in this chapter. Set a date to work through the five R's of repentance this week. What do you need to do to turn back on the path toward God?

Rocket Prayer

"Lord, help me turn toward you."

Say this prayer when you feel resistant to repentance. Say this prayer when you aren't sure where you've made left turns. Say this prayer when you begin the repentance process and find yourself fearing the discomfort of release and reconciliation. Say it when you're at a crossroad. Remember that the Lord is faithful to forgive and will welcome you back to his path with open arms every time.

Prayer of Response

Before you close this workbook for the rest of the week, take a few minutes to write a prayer of response to God. First, thank him for ways he has been good to you. Then, tell him what you're thinking and feeling as you process what you've learned.

Pass It On

When your child wrongs you, a sibling, or a friend, don't simply force an empty apology. Take the time to help him understand what he did. After all, your child can't repent if he can't identify his own sin. Ask him reflection questions to guide him through identifying how his actions hurt someone else and rejected God's teaching. (For a good example of guiding questions, revisit the example I shared in the Pass It On section of chapter 3.) If your child appears hard-hearted, focus on the broken relationship that their action created by asking questions like "What is your relationship with your sister like right now?" and "How did this day change after you called your friend stupid?"

When your child has done something wrong and wants to repent, help her do so thoroughly using the five R's. First, she needs to ask for and accept God's forgiveness. Then, it's time to confess and seek forgiveness from her brother. Finally, she should do what she can to make it right—for instance, she might need to give up some of her allowance money to help replace a toy she broke. Even fairly young children can learn that repentance isn't just about saying "sorry."

Also, be intentional about modeling repentance for your children. Sometimes this means allowing your children to see you repent to others, like Don did with our youngest daughter, Cammy, when he repented to Mac. (She has never forgotten that experience.) Other times, this means repenting to your children. After all, they're probably the ones you wrong the most. When you lose your temper or make a selfish choice that hurts your kids, confess your sin to them and seek their forgiveness.

11

the freedom of forgiveness

Forgive anyone who offends you.
Remember, the Lord forgave you, so you must forgive others.

COLOSSIANS 3:13

At that same conference in Uganda where I met Claudia in 2007, I taught a session called "Forgiving the Men in Your Lives." Afterward, a young woman named Sylvia timidly approached and asked if we could talk. I found a chair for each of us, and we went outside to sit in the shade.

"When I was fifteen years old, my father sold me for eight cows to an older man I hated," she said. "Do I have to forgive my father?"

There was pain in her eyes and pleading in her voice. I sent up a quick prayer for wisdom. "Yes, Sylvia," I said, "if you want freedom, you must forgive your father." Tears welled up in her eyes, and she folded her hands and bowed her head. She grimaced as she confessed her grudge and asked the Lord to forgive her for the bitterness she'd harbored. Then she said, "I forgive my father."

After a period of silence, she looked up and said, "Though I had five children with him, my husband didn't love me, and he beat me. I was his second wife. He had sex with women in town, then came home and wanted sex from me, too. Do I have to forgive my husband?" I took a slow breath and sent up another prayer asking for wisdom. "Yes, Sylvia," I said, "God wants you to forgive your husband."

She began to cry softly and bowed her head again. "Lord, please forgive me for the anger and bitterness that I have held against my husband." She sighed. "I forgive my husband."

There was another long silence before she spoke again. "I moved away from my husband, rented a little hut, and got a job as a secretary. I couldn't afford to send my children to school, so they stayed home while I was at work. One day while I was gone, a neighbor came over and raped my three-year-old daughter and gave her AIDS. She died eighteen months ago." I dreaded the question I knew she was about to ask. With tears in my eyes, I pleaded with the Lord to give me the right words. I felt anger on Sylvia's behalf—so much that I wanted to get revenge on that man myself. But I knew that wasn't God's will.

She asked, "Do I have to forgive the man who raped and murdered my daughter?"

By this time, tears were running down my face, too. "Yes," I whispered, "you need to forgive the man who raped and murdered your daughter."

Sylvia immediately bowed her head. "Lord, please forgive me for harboring unforgiveness toward the man who raped and murdered my daughter. I forgive him."

Personal Reflection

How do you feel about Sylvia's forgiveness? Why?

To this day, I feel emotional when I think about Sylvia's story, and I'll be honest: some of that emotion is anger. I felt it the day she shared her story, and I feel it when I retell it now. Maybe you're feeling it, too: that deep, unsettled sense of injustice and a desire to see it made right. Maybe forgiveness feels unreasonable or even unfair. You don't want to see that man's behavior condoned or forgotten, and you certainly don't want to see him be allowed to do the same act again.

But here's the thing: forgiveness doesn't mean condoning the wrong. It doesn't mean forgetting the wrong happened. It doesn't mean allowing it to continue. Forgiveness doesn't even mean giving up that desire for justice. It simply means turning your right to justice over to Jesus, the ultimate authority and source of justice.

Personal Reflection

Read Jesus's parable about forgiveness in Matthew 18:23–34.

What is your takeaway?

When we harbor unforgiveness against someone, we are essentially demanding payment from that person, even if we don't articulate that to them. In *The Secrets of Lasting Forgiveness*, Bruce Wilkinson describes unforgiveness as locking that person away in a debtor's prison in our heart until they pay restitution. But we owe Jesus far more than any person owes us—even more than the rapist owes Sylvia. We owe him everything. And therefore, everything that is owed to us is actually owed to Jesus.

When we forgive, the debt doesn't go away. It simply gets passed on to the one who is truly owed, and he will handle it as he sees fit. Jesus is our Judge and our Defender, seated at the right hand of God, and he is the only one with the right to enact justice. Our choice to forgive honors his role as the ultimate master. Our submission removes barriers between us and Jesus and frees us to thrive in his peace.

You see, forgiveness isn't for the sake of the other person. It has nothing to do with whether they deserve it or have even apologized. Forgiveness is for us, and it is for Jesus.

Personal Reflection

Take a minute to pray. Thank Jesus for the great sacrifice he made in order to forgive you.

Now, consider your own unforgiveness. Are there any grudges that immediately come to mind? Write them below.

According to Scripture, unforgiveness is a serious matter, and it's important that we talk about the consequences. In Matthew 18, Jesus concludes the parable of the two debtors by saying the king threw his servant into prison to be tortured after learning the man (whom he forgave) had not extended forgiveness to his peer. Then, in verse 35, Jesus said this: "That's what my heavenly Father will do to you if you refuse to forgive your brothers and sisters from your heart."

Ouch. Torture? That's not what we expect from a loving God. What are we supposed to do with that language? There are two ways to think about this. First, in an eternal sense. Unforgiveness is sin—Jesus is clear about that. And it's a sin that's particularly personal to God, because refusing to forgive someone is the ultimate snub at the sacrifice Jesus made to forgive us. By refusing to forgive, we make a choice to walk down the sinful path instead of God's path, despite his constant and loving invitation to take us back. And the sinful path does not lead to heaven.

The second way to think about this torture is more immediate and (hopefully) temporary. When I ask women with forgiveness issues how they feel, many times they say they feel "tormented." Bitterness is consuming and miserable. It gets in the way of other relationships and causes stress and anxiety. It makes us do things we don't want to do, such as gossip or seek revenge. It prevents us from enjoying life and feeling free.

When we spiral into bitterness, we literally build our own prison. We put up walls around ourselves to protect us from other people, but those walls only trap us. We revisit the unforgiven wrong in our minds over and over again, lashing ourselves with it like a whip. Unforgiveness itself is torture for us—a reality that hopefully prompts us to leave it behind.

Personal Reflection

Consider the grudges you hold. How has that unforgiveness led to torment in your life?

Now, sometimes this torture is hard to pinpoint. Not that it isn't there or isn't powerful in our life, but it isn't easy to connect to unforgiveness. It may show up in our life as anxiety, chronic pain, apathy, or cynicism—symptoms we blame on other sources or write off as part of our personality. Often, it isn't until we forgive that we see just how oppressive our unforgiveness was.

Years ago, my friend Mandy came to me for advice navigating family tension. As we talked, it became clear she harbored some serious grudges. She could name every wrong her family had done, and she was bitter about each one. With a little help, Mandy came to see how she'd repeatedly hurt them, too, and she decided she wanted to forgive and be set free from her bitterness. After two and a half hours of prayer and tears, Mandy opened her eyes and said with surprise, "I'm completely at peace." Then she stood up and touched her back, even more surprised. "My back doesn't hurt anymore!" Mandy's unforgiveness had caused stress and tension in her life, and it had manifested as tight and achy muscles. She'd never have guessed unforgiveness was the cause of her pain, but that day she experienced amazing release—in her heart *and* her back.

Sylvia, too, was surprised by the healing that came with forgiveness. Like Mandy, she expressed an immediate sense of freedom after she prayed to forgive the men in her life. "The blackness in me is gone," she told me. "I feel like a burden has been lifted." A few weeks later, she sent me an email sharing new insight: "I had been so heavy with unforgiveness that I didn't have the energy to even parent my children," she wrote. "I would come home from work, lay down on the floor of our hut, go to sleep, and ignore my children. Now, I have been freed, and I can again be a mom to my children." Praise the Lord! He had set her free.

Personal Reflection

How have you seen heartfelt forgiveness lead to freedom, whether in your own life or the life of a friend or family member?

Take a moment to pray. Thank God that he desires healing for you, and ask him to help you choose healing over your unforgiveness.

It's important to note that everything in this chapter so far is true even when the person we need to forgive is ourselves. Whether we've hurt someone else or failed to live up to our own standards, harboring unforgiveness toward ourselves is just as problematic as harboring it against someone else. It still causes us to spiral in unhealthy ways. It still snubs Jesus's sacrifice. It still denies Jesus his role as the rightful owner of the debt.

Personal Reflection

In what way are you harboring unforgiveness toward yourself? Jesus wants you to forgive yourself. He forgives you.

It's almost time to walk through the process of forgiveness together. But first, let's consider a few lies that might be getting in your way:

"It happened so long ago, I've just put it out of my mind." Wounds don't go away without forgiveness. They are still there and will continue to affect your life until you repent of bitterness and forgive.

"I am not suffering because of unforgiveness." Remember that this suffering can be hard to identify. You might blame anxiety, personality, health issues, or traumatic circumstances for the torment that may actually be caused by unforgiveness. You might even be so blind to it that you think everything is great—even when it could be so much better.

"I can forgive others, but I can't forgive myself." Jesus already paid the price for your sin. By harboring unforgiveness against yourself, you are not only denying yourself the freedom he has invited you to, but you are insulting him by suggesting that more needs to be done. He is waiting to hold you and heal your heart.

"I've done this so many times that I can't be forgiven again." His death covered all your sins—past, present, and future. As you forgive yourself and keep your eyes on him, he can give you the strength to overcome habitual sin.

"They won't receive my forgiveness." They may not. But remember: forgiveness isn't about them. It's about you and Jesus. Also, unlike repentance, forgiveness isn't something you necessarily need to articulate to the other person. Communicating your forgiveness to someone is often an incredibly powerful and healing act for both parties, but there are some cases where it might not be wise. Ask God for guidance on this, and follow the Holy Spirit's prompting. If you aren't sure, talk about it with your mentor.

"If I forgive, it means I'm a pushover." When we hold on to unforgiveness, we give the wrongdoers indefinite power over us. We allow their wrong to continue hurting and controlling us. But when we forgive, we set ourselves free from that wrong. When we forgive, we claim victory in Christ over all injustice. There's nothing weak about that.

In regard to that final lie, it's important to say that forgiving someone does not mean rolling over and allowing someone to continue mistreating you. If you have someone in your life who is wounding you repeatedly—whether it's your mother overstepping appropriate boundaries or your husband routinely belittling you—talk to your mentor about the situation. She'll help you start with forgiveness, then make a plan to effectively deal with the problem.

Personal Reflection

Which lies in this list resonate with you?

Can you identify any other lies getting in the way of forgiveness in your life?

It's time to forgive. You have been in a prison of your own making for too long, and the Lord is waiting to heal and free your heart. Holding other people in a prison does not give you power over them or over the hurt that was done to you—it only weighs you down, weakens your current relationships, and prevents you from experiencing genuine peace.

Personal Action

Pull out the timeline you made in chapter 9. Read through it. Write down the name of anyone who wounded you, along with a word or phrase to remind you of the specific ways they hurt you. You may want to use your journal for this.

When you're done writing the names that appear in your timeline, take a few minutes to consider who else you might need to forgive. Who else in your past stirs up feelings of bitterness?

By the end of this week, your task it to carve out time to pray through this list, offense by offense, and release each one to Jesus. Some of you may be excited to get these weights off your chest, but I imagine many of you are struggling to feel ready. As you prepare, here are a couple of things to think about:

First, I encourage you to spend a good amount of time in prayer. Ask the Lord to make you more like him by giving you a heart of forgiveness. Process aloud with the Lord the hang-ups that are getting in your way, but don't hem and haw over whether you're ready to forgive. If Sylvia or Claudia had dwelt too much on whether to forgive the people who had hurt them, they may not have been able to do so. Instead, they immediately obeyed God's command.

Second, I strongly suggest that you consider inviting your mentor or another trusted and mature confidante into the process. Just like Sylvia and Mandy talked about their wounds with me and prayed their forgiveness in my presence, choosing to welcome someone else into your forgiveness provides an element of accountability. They might help you see things in a new light, and they'll be able to catch you if you start justifying yourself instead of extending forgiveness. Having another person involved in this process also enhances the healing you experience, because studies show that talking about traumatic experiences with someone actually helps your brain heal from that trauma.

Third, if you have very recently been wounded in a traumatic way, I recognize that you might not be ready for this. That's OK. I have seen friends lose children and endure abuse, and I understand that it takes time for the fog to clear before you can even think clearly. The important thing right now is that you cling to God in your pain instead of shutting him out. Instead of jumping right into this exercise, take time to talk with your mentor about this trauma. Also, pray that the Lord will help you move toward forgiveness, and listen for his instructions. I have found that the Lord always calls me to forgive before I personally feel ready. It is an act of faith and worship.

Personal Action

Carve out at least one to two hours that you can dedicate to uninterrupted and undistracted time praying through your list. If you've invited someone else into this process, coordinate schedules with them. Choose a private place, and make sure you have a box of tissues on hand.

I suggest you start with the person you have the most unforgiveness toward, then pray through the rest of your list. For each individual offense, start by asking the Lord to forgive you for harboring unforgiveness. Then, just like Sylvia did, open your heart and clearly state your forgiveness. For example, "Lord, please forgive me for harboring bitterness and unforgiveness toward Tyler for cheating on me in high school. I forgive Tyler for his unfaithfulness and release him from my heart's prison."

If it's helpful, use that example as a template and simply fill in the correct name and offense. After you've said these words, conjure an image of that person in your mind, and speak your forgiveness directly to them. ("Tyler, I forgive you completely.") This last step might feel silly, but it's actually incredibly powerful.

When you come to people on your list who have hurt you in multiple ways, take time to go through the process with each individual wound. While it's tempting to say, "I forgive my mother for everything she's done," it's essential that you articulate each offense—even if it makes you emotional. This is what it takes to fully forgive.

If you reach a person or an offense that you cannot forgive, stop and cry out to the Lord for help. Ask him to help you see that person as he sees them. Ask him to open your heart and give you Christ's love for them. Wait, and continue praying. It can take several minutes to feel your heart soften. If you absolutely cannot get to a point of genuine forgiveness toward that person, follow up with your mentor or a counselor.

Personal Reflection

How do you feel after forgiving all these offenses?

When Mandy forgave, she felt freedom in her heart and relief in her back. When Sylvia forgave, she felt a huge burden lift, and she was able to be more present and engaged with her children than she had been in years. Claudia, too—who we met in the previous chapter—experienced amazing healing when she forgave the enemy tribe who had tormented her people and brutally murdered her cousin. With her bitterness gone, Claudia was able to hold hands with women from the enemy tribe and pray with them, helping them grow closer to Jesus through repentance. When they repented of the harm their tribe had done, she was able to honestly reconcile with them. And when they had finished praying, Claudia invited those women and their families to stay in her small home while they were in town.

> **PARENTING TIP**
> *Develop a habit of asking your children for forgiveness when you mess up. Modeling forgiveness is the best way to instill it in your kids.*

You see, those women had walked twelve miles with their families in order to attend the conference.

And, because the village was enemy territory, they were camping outside of town where they were exposed to poisonous snakes and other dangerous animals. Because of Claudia's forgiveness, not only did she experience personal freedom, but she helped others know Jesus better and protected young families from danger. Because of her forgiveness, former enemies slept under one roof and decades-long strife between tribes began to break down.

You have done a hard thing this week. But you can have faith that the Lord will do amazing things in you and those around you because of it.

Rocket Prayer

"Lord, I forgive them because you forgave me first."

Say this prayer when your children irritate you. Say it when someone cuts in front of you in the grocery checkout line or speeds around you on the highway. Say it when your husband makes an insensitive comment that hurts your feelings. By developing a heart of forgiveness, we avoid ever building new prisons.

Prayer of Response

Before you close this workbook for the rest of the week, take a few minutes to write a prayer of response to God. First, thank him for ways he has been good to you. Then, tell him what you're thinking and feeling as you process what you've learned.

Pass It On

When you tuck your children into bed at night, ask them to think about a moment in the day when they had to ask for forgiveness because of something they did wrong. Help them say a short prayer to thank Jesus for forgiving them.

When another child apologizes to your son or daughter (whether it's a friend or a sibling), help them extend genuine forgiveness. If their tone tells you that they don't really forgive the other child, ask them some guiding questions to help them get there. For instance, ask them to remember a time they hurt someone else and had to ask for forgiveness. How would they have felt if that child had not forgiven them?

If your child is old enough, share with them an appropriate story of how you forgave someone in your own life. (For example, forgiving a friend or family member who snapped at you or said something unkind.) Your children watch you closely, and they'll pay attention to how your forgiveness affects the relationship.

LIVING A NEW WAY

THREE WEEKS

Now that we've cleared the way by righting our priorities, growing in relationship with the Lord, and freeing ourselves from baggage, we will explore specific ways to live life in a new, godly fashion.

taking control of your thoughts

Take every thought captive to obey Christ.

2 CORINTHIANS 10:5 (ESV)

I never thought I'd be climbing one of the world's largest mountains. But there I was, in the middle of the night, putting one foot in front of the other near the top of Tanzania's Mount Kilimanjaro. It was 2016, and though it wasn't on my bucket list, I'd agreed to summit the highest mountain in Africa on International Women's Day to raise awareness about the violence committed against women in war zones around the world—particularly in parts of central Africa, where rape was being used as a weapon in war.

It was summit day, which means we started the day's climb at midnight so we could make it to the top and then descend to a safe level before nightfall. I was third in the line of climbers. In the dark, I was alone with my thoughts, and they weren't pretty. After days of climbing and camping, I was indescribably exhausted. My altitude sickness was causing nausea, diarrhea, headaches, and dizziness. I felt like I was climbing a mountain with a severe case of the flu. *Everything hurts,* I thought. *This forty-pound pack seems like ninety. How could I possibly have to poop again? I feel like I'm going to puke. I wish I was tucked into my king-size bed. This parka makes me feel like my head is in a cave. Man, this is steep. What if I don't make it? I'll let everyone down.* Needless to say, I was not exactly optimistic. My mind swirled with negative thoughts and complaints.

Personal Reflection

Describe a time recently when your thoughts seemed to spiral out of control.

I needed to snap out of it. If I was going to reach the top of that mountain, I had to get control of my thoughts. Thinking about my misery wasn't going to help me reach my goal. So, I focused all my mental energy on my steps: right, left, right, left. I watched the guide's feet ahead of me and matched his stride. I paid attention to the crunch of the lava rocks beneath my boots and the swishing sound my oxygen tank made with each breath. As the storm of worries began to fade, I replaced them with worshipful prayers. *Lord, you are mighty*, I prayed silently. *You have a good plan. Thank you for being here with me. Thank you for giving me good health so I can do this.* Feeling renewed, I began to sing praise songs in my head to the beat of my steps. Everything else faded away.

That day, my purpose was to reach the top of Mount Kilimanjaro for the sake of vulnerable women, and to do it, I had to take control of my thoughts. The same is true in life. We have a life purpose, and our thoughts either help us fulfill that purpose or they pull us away.

Personal Reflection

Turn back to the first chapter of this workbook and locate your life purpose statement. Rewrite it here. If you'd like to make changes based on what you've learned in this workbook, feel free to do so.

Locate your mom job description, which is also in chapter 1. This is an important secondary purpose. Rewrite your job description here.

It's common to think of thoughts as harmless. As long as we don't say that judgmental remark out loud or act on that temptation, everything is fine, right? Well, not exactly. Our thought life, left unchecked, has a serious effect on the rest of our life—even when we do a decent job keeping those thoughts in our head in the short term.

In Matthew 5:21–22, Jesus said, "You have heard that our ancestors were told, 'You must not murder. If you commit murder, you are subject to judgment.' But I say, if you are even angry with someone, you are subject to judgment!" A few verses later he said, "You have heard the commandment that says, 'You must not commit adultery.' But I say, anyone who even looks at a woman with lust has already committed adultery with her in his heart." According to Jesus, our thoughts clearly aren't harmless. To him, we're just as accountable for our thoughts as we are for our actions. That's not just some strict and arbitrary rule. God made us and knows how we work. He knows that our thoughts influence our lives and need to be taken seriously if we're to thrive.

Think back to the story I told in chapter 8 about the summer I worked biffy duty under the tyranny of Jamie. When I made a choice to stay at camp and surrender to Jamie's injustice, I committed to submit to her with a good attitude because I believed that's what the Lord wanted me to do. Nevertheless, it was incredibly difficult to respond submissively when she punished me unjustly—especially in front of others—and I constantly had to keep my thoughts in check. If I'd allowed myself to complain or back-talk Jamie in my head, there's no way I'd have made it through the summer without shifting into a seriously bad attitude. Those thoughts would have festered and made me bitter. Instead, when thoughts of self-pity or rebellion popped into my head, I had to reject them immediately and replace them with positive thoughts that kept me focused on serving God.

You see, our minds are like a gateway. All kinds of thoughts show up at the gate, and we don't necessarily have control over which thoughts come knocking. But we do have control over which thoughts we let in.

Personal Reflection

Broadly speaking, what kind of negative thoughts do you frequently allow inside? Thoughts of self-pity or complaint? Worry about the future? Obsession over an offense? Criticism of others? Criticism of yourself?

List a few specific ungodly trains of thought that regularly run on repeat in your brain.

How have those negative thoughts affected your attitudes and actions?

Think about your life purpose. How do those negative thoughts keep you from living into that purpose in daily life?

Here's the reality: what you allow through the gate gets access to your heart, and it has very real and practical implications for your life.

For example, let's say you have a habit of mentally criticizing your husband for being lazy. Even if you don't say that criticism out loud, it won't be long before it seeps into your heart. You'll be quicker to feel irritated with him, and you'll start perceiving more and more of his actions (or inactions) as lazy, even if his behavior is perfectly reasonable. You'll nullify his perspective on situations, and you'll even stop appreciating his positive qualities.

The same is true for the way we think about our children, our friends, ourselves, our circumstances, and God. The thoughts we allow through the gate get down into our heart. If those thoughts are good and honoring to the Lord, they help you grow closer to him and become more like him, and they improve your relationships with others and your outlook on life. But if they are sinful, they harden your heart and make it hard for you to hear and feel the Holy Spirit, and they can hurt your relationships with others and lead to bad attitudes.

Personal Action

Read Proverbs 4:23: "Guard your heart above all else, for it determines the course of your life." Allow it to sink deeply into your heart.

Use the space below to journal as a prayer to God. Repent for the ways you've failed to guard your heart and ask God's forgiveness. Ask him to help you "take every thought captive," as Paul said in 2 Corinthians.

Getting control of our thoughts isn't just about rejecting the ungodly ideas that show up at our gate. It's also about welcoming and encouraging the ones that will move our heart toward the Lord. For many of us, the thoughts we're best at chasing away are actually the ones that come from the Holy Spirit—the thoughts that tell us to go talk to the lonely older neighbor, that the money we're about to spend on new shoes could be used to provide for someone in need, that the selfless thing to do would be to take the trash out ourselves this time. We chase these thoughts away the minute they show up at our gate because we don't want to sacrifice our selfishness or even think deeply about uncomfortable things, such as how God calls us to spend our time and money.

Personal Reflection

Broadly speaking, describe the kinds of holy thoughts you often push aside.

Describe a specific time recently when you pushed a holy thought out of your mind because facing it was uncomfortable.

Use the space below to journal a prayer to God. Repent for ignoring those holy thoughts and ask how he wants you to engage more fully with things he cares about.

So, what does it actually look like to get control of your thought life? The apostle Paul said it best: "take every thought captive" (2 Corinthians 10:5, ESV). As new thoughts approach your gate day in and day out, practice grabbing and looking at each one. Ask yourself if giving that thought access to your heart will help you live into your life purpose or detract from it.

For example, when a worry starts to creep in, ask yourself, "Will fretting about this help me love the Lord and raise godly children?" If the answer is no, tell that worry to get out.

Now, I understand how difficult it is to keep unwelcome thoughts away. Worry, jealousy, judgment, self-pity, and all the other unhelpful thoughts are downright relentless. The key is to intentionally replace those thoughts with Scripture, prayer, and worship. That way, your mind is busy with good things. For instance, when a worry comes knocking at your gate, you might recite a relevant Scripture verse, such as Proverbs 3:5–6: "Trust in the LORD with all your heart; do not depend on your own understanding. Seek his will in all you do, and he will show you which path to take." Then, sing a worship song in your head. Or, you might send up a rocket prayer asking for the Lord's help in that moment, then turn your mind to praying for other people—say, five friends or family members. There is something about

> **PARENTING TIP**
> *When your kids say something mean or lash out in anger, calmly ask questions about the thoughts they were having. This helps them learn to be more aware of their thought life.*

interceding for others that calms our heart and focuses our mind. This approach is better than simply trying to control your mind with positive self-talk because it invites the Holy Spirit to actually change the way you think and feel. From there, you'll notice that more positive and constructive thoughts come to mind naturally.

Personal Action

Pick at least one of the verses below and write it on an index card. Tape it somewhere you'll see it daily, and work toward memorizing the words. They'll come in handy when you need to chase away negative thoughts.

1 Thessalonians 5:18: "Be thankful in all circumstances, for this is God's will for you."

Proverbs 3:5–6: "Trust in the LORD with all your heart; do not depend on your own understanding. Seek his will in all you do, and he will show you which path to take."

Isaiah 41:10: "Don't be afraid, for I am with you. Don't be discouraged, for I am your God."

Ephesians 3:20: "Now all glory to God, who is able, through his mighty power at work within us, to accomplish infinitely more than we might ask or think."

At first, rejecting and chasing away all those unholy thoughts can feel like a huge undertaking. Give yourself grace, and know that it takes a lot of practice to hone this skill. For now, it's enough that you pay attention to the Holy Spirit. With time, you'll likely find that those kinds of thoughts come less and less. It's like they realize they're no longer welcome.

Personal Reflection

Take a look at the list you made earlier of specific ungodly thoughts that are common for you. Pick three, and rewrite them here.

For each negative thought, add a verse (and maybe a song) you can use in the moment to chase that thought away. You can use the verses above or others.

As you practice rejecting ungodly thoughts, remember also to welcome the holy ones. When you ask yourself if a thought helps you live into your purpose and the answer is yes, pay attention. Welcome that thought inside. Explore the idea with God through prayer, and maybe bring it up with a friend, your spouse, or your children to discuss further.

For example, let's say you are shopping online for a new rug. A thought comes to your minds gate saying you don't need a new rug right now and you could use the money to provide for someone in need instead. You feel tempted to reject that thought, but you concede that it's a godly thought and welcome it in. You pray about it, and the Holy Spirit confirms that he wants you to use that money in a charitable way. So, instead of dwelling on rug styles, you put your mental energy toward developing a short list of options for how to donate that money. Then, over dinner, you tell the kids about your conviction and invite them to help you decide what to do with the money. In this way, that holy thought not only changed your heart by making you more generous, but also spilled over to your kids. Now that's a win-win.

Personal Reflection

Take a look at the question you answered earlier about a holy thought you recently chased away. How will you welcome that thought into your heart next time? What would God want you to do? How could you invite others into it?

As you work hard this week to take every thought captive, never forget God's love and grace for you. We're not taking control of our thought lives in order to win his love or meet some arbitrary standard. We're working hard to take control of our thoughts because doing so draws us into a deeper love relationship with the Lord. God knows how much thoughts affect our hearts and our lives, and like a good parent, he is teaching us how to thrive.

So if you feel shame this week when you inevitably let bad thoughts through your gate or reject holy ones, know that God is not up there somewhere shaking his head, wondering why you can't get it together. That's not who our God is. Our God is a giver of infinite grace, and he knows we can only manage one baby step at a time. Let thoughts of guilt, shame, or self-criticism be ones you reject at the gate this week, because they have no place in your heart.

Rocket Prayer

"Lord, I give you control of my mind."

Say this prayer when unholy thoughts pop into your mind and you need help chasing them away. Say this prayer when good but uncomfortable thoughts come to the gate and you need God's help to let them in. By choosing to give God control of our thoughts, we are leaning into our life purpose to love God with all our heart, soul, strength, and *mind*.

Prayer of Response

Before you close this workbook for the rest of the week, take a few minutes to write a prayer of response to God. First, thank him for ways he has been good to you. Then, tell him what you're thinking and feeling as you process what you've learned.

Pass It On

Consider passing on what you've learned this week by choosing to thoughtfully engage with your child when you notice her thoughts spinning out of control. For example, let's say your daughter is a perfectionist and tends to get worked up when homework or an art project doesn't go just right. The next time you witness her starting to panic over an imperfect drawing, stop what you're doing and get on her level. Use questions to help her process the situation herself. Your side of the conversation might look like this: "Hey, Julie, I can see you're upset. What are you feeling right now? Why do you think you feel mad? I get that—I tend to get upset when I mess up, too. Now tell me: when you started this, what were you trying to create? That sounds amazing. Now I know you're feeling anxious and mad, but I want you to think about something: how does Jesus feel about you? Yes, he loves you no matter what. Do you think obsessing about this mistake and beating yourself up will change that? Let's take a break from your artwork and talk to the Lord about this." Pray with her, then put on some praise music and dance together. Ask her how her heart feels different after shifting her focus to the Lord, then encourage her to resume her project with a new perspective.

You can also have these kinds of conversations in retrospect. Use the same kind of guiding questions to help your child reflect on a moment during the week when his anxiety spiraled out of control. Help him decide in advance to go to the Lord with his worries the next time they come, and help him learn to pray with words that describe how powerful God is. The goal is for him to understand that his anxious thoughts don't have control—God does.

living an honest life

The crooked heart will not prosper;
the lying tongue tumbles into trouble.

PROVERBS 17:20

When my friend Victoria was young, it was clear to her that she was the least favorite child in the household. While her father doted on her siblings, he spoke to Victoria with contempt or indifference. He frequently snapped at her, and when she misbehaved, he exploded with anger—something he never did with the other kids. Even her mother treated her differently, tending to ignore Victoria while engaging intently with her siblings. Victoria felt invisible, and she couldn't figure out what she'd done to make her parents dislike her so much.

Years later, she learned from another family member that her dad, Ben, wasn't really her biological father. She had been conceived during an affair. The news made her head spin—but it all began to make sense. Of course her dad looked at her with disdain, and of course her mom was careful not to show her any favor. Her mom had told lie after lie in an attempt to cover up the infidelity, but Ben clearly knew the truth. By continuing to stick to her lie, Victoria's mom prevented reconciliation and unity in the family—and Victoria, now in her forties, still lives with the scars from bearing the brunt of that brokenness and deception.

Personal Reflection

Describe a time you discovered lies that your friends or family had been keeping from you.

How did those lies affect you and others?

We all know—at least in theory—that lying is wrong. We know it hurts people, like Victoria's mother deeply hurt her husband and her daughter. We know that the Bible clearly calls us to be truthful people. In Leviticus, God lays out standards for how his people should behave, including that they should not lie or deceive one another.

In Proverbs 12:22, we see that "The LORD detests lying lips, but he delights in those who tell the truth." In John 8:44, Jesus calls Satan "the father of lies." Clearly, Jesus takes even the smallest deceit seriously.

> **PARENTING TIP**
> *Always take your children's dishonesty seriously—even when it's a cute little white lie.*

Yet, despite innately knowing that lying is wrong, few of us truly live honest lives—and it's getting in the way of our relationships, inner health, and efforts to be Foundational parents. We fib to get out of trouble or to avoid inconvenient conversations with our families. We build webs of lies in an attempt to cover up secrets. And often, without actually telling a lie, we intentionally misrepresent ourselves, our motives, or our actions.

You see, when I talk about lying or dishonesty in this chapter, I'm not simply talking about the act of telling a boldface lie. Many times, our deceit is much more nuanced than that. It's the act of hiding something, adjusting the truth, or simply omitting information. These are lies too. Often these lies are over small, seemingly inconsequential things.

So why do we lie? Most of the time, dishonesty comes out of a desire to protect ourselves from the consequences of our sin or hide our shame. Most of us are not being dishonest because we want to hurt someone else or because we get a thrill out of the lie. We're doing it to cover something up—just like Don lied to his mom as a child to cover up the fact that he tried to break into someone's house for a piece of candy.

In some cases, that something we're hiding feels like a dark, secret part of our life that no one sees. These things can be a big deal, such as infidelity, a gambling habit, fraud, an eating disorder, abuse toward our children or another family member, or addiction to alcohol, drugs, or pornography. It can also be something less extreme, such as dealing with depression, hoarding junk in your garage, overindulging on sweets when no one is around, or refusing to tell anyone a secret from your past that still weighs on you. What binds all of these possibilities together is the fact that they create a sense of ongoing secrecy, or what I call a "secret life." Living this way causes shame, fear, and isolation. It cuts you off from the help we all need from others, and it creates a massive gulf between you and God and the people around you.

If you feel like you are living a secret life, take it seriously and deal with it. Talk to your mentor or your counselor. Even if it doesn't feel like a big deal now, secret lives can spiral out of control quicker and more dramatically than we imagine. I have a friend whose teenage daughter, Karina, had a relationship with a stranger online that she kept secret from her family. In the end, Karina ended up married to a gun dealer who abuses her and their children and bars her from having any communication with her family. She has become a prisoner in her own house. It seemed like an innocent online relationship, and she could never have imagined what her secret life would lead to. Neither can you. What's a habit now could become an addiction. What's a seemingly harmless indulgence could someday bankrupt you or lead to serious illness.

Personal Reflection

If you have a secret life—either big or small—name the thing you are hiding.

Spend a few minutes journaling as a prayer to God. Remember, none of your secret is news to him, so you can be totally honest. Tell God how this dishonesty is affecting your life and those around you, and ask him to give you the courage to come out of hiding.

Now, name one person—ideally a mentor, pastor, counselor, or spouse—who you'd like to be honest with. Make a commitment to schedule time with that person this week and share the truth with them.

On a daily basis, most of our deceit comes down to one-off lies. For example, we might apologetically tell a boss we misunderstood an assignment in order to cover up the shame we feel for doing an unsatisfactory job. We might hide the evidence of a recent shopping spree from our spouse to avoid conflict over our spending. We might tell a sister-in-law that her birthday present is in the mail when, in reality, we completely forgot her birthday until seeing the reminder on Facebook.

Of course, the reality is that these kinds of lies are rarely actually one-offs. They're almost always part of a larger pattern of obscuring the truth in order to avoid consequences or improve the way others perceive us—even if that pattern doesn't quite rise to the level of a secret life.

Personal Reflection

Describe a time or two recently when you told a lie, obscured the truth, or hid information (or shopping bags) in order to cover up something you did.

The crazy thing is that most of us continue this pattern of deceit because we believe lies *about lying*. Let's explore some of those lies.

"I'm not hurting anyone." Lying always damages relationships because it creates distance and blocks communication. It builds walls in our spiritual lives as well as in our human relationships. Plus, when your children notice your lies (which they will), they'll learn from you that it's OK to be dishonest—and that hurts them in the long run.

"I need to protect myself." Be honest with yourself: you're trying to protect yourself from the consequences of your own choices. Back it up one step: if you hadn't gossiped about a friend, there would be no consequences to protect yourself from. That is where your focus needs to be.

Note: In rare and extreme circumstances, it may be acceptable to lie in order to protect yourself or someone else from legitimate danger. In Scripture, we see that God blessed the midwives who lied to Pharaoh in order to save the lives of Hebrew babies. If you find yourself in a situation when lying could save you, your children, or someone else from physical harm, send up a rocket prayer and do what you think is wise. Also, if you're in a physically abusive relationship, get out now. Don't wait for a situation to arise when you have to lie to save you or your child from being beaten or killed. Talk to your mentor if you question your situation.

"If I tell the truth, it will hurt the relationship." Yes, it might. But telling the truth isn't what truly hurt the relationship—the action you tried to cover up is what hurt the relationship, and that's already done. You are just trying to delay the consequences by lying. Commitment to honesty is the greatest deterrent to doing wrong. If you are committed to being honest, you'll think long and hard before doing something that would require an uncomfortable confession.

"I told the truth—I just left out part of it." A half-truth is a lie. Remember, dishonesty isn't just about boldface lies. It's about misrepresenting the truth. When you omit information, you misrepresent yourself, your motivations, or your actions.

"Lying is easier than facing the consequences." It might feel that way now, but in the long run coming clean is a much better choice. First of all, if you get caught in your lie, the consequences will likely be worse than if you chose to confess. Second, lying itself comes with heavy consequences—something we'll talk about shortly.

Personal Reflection

Which lies in the list above resonate with you the most?

Can you identify other lies you believe about lying? If so, take a few minutes to write how you are going to counter those lies.

In the previous chapter, we learned that our thoughts—which many of us used to view as harmless—actually have a serious effect on our lives. Deceit is the same way. Deceiving someone is a sin, and while we want to believe that a sin just disappears after a while even if we don't repent, it does not. Each dishonesty is like a brick. Brick by brick we build an impenetrable wall around ourselves that affects our spiritual and interpersonal relationships. The hiding spot might feel safe at times, but ultimately it cuts us off from genuine relationships with others, making us unable to truly know someone else or be known by them. In the end, we're trapped by our wall with nothing but our own shame for company—and this is not what our loving Father wants for any of his children.

Our dishonesty also affects other people. In some serious cases, the outer effects on others are obvious. We squander our money, ruin our marriages, neglect our children, take what isn't ours, and cause emotional pain to our friends and family. But the smaller, mundane dishonesties affect others, too, because our brick wall creates a noticeable feeling of distance. Our children, spouses, friends, and family are left feeling shut out and disconnected, which is deeply hurtful. Living in a dishonest way also teaches our children that dishonesty is normal and acceptable—perpetuating the cycle for another generation.

God calls us to take down the brick wall with repentance and forgiveness so that we can experience the freedom that comes with an honest life—so that there's nothing between us and God's strong foundation. In an honest life, there are no walls separating you from God or others. Your relationships can be deep, genuine, and fulfilling. In an honest life, you are not weighed down by shame or fear of exposure. You can be who you were created to be, because you were designed for a life of freedom.

Personal Reflection

What emotions does the idea of living an honest life stir up in you?

If you find yourself feeling nervous or agitated, consider why. Would living an honest life require you to come clean about something you've been hiding? How would you have to present yourself differently at work or with friends and family?

Read Proverbs 2:7–8.

Write a sentence personalizing God's promise to you. (For example, "If I live an honest life, God promises to _____.")

So, how do we break free of our deceitful habits and start living an honest life? Well, for starters, we have to wipe the slate clean. You simply cannot begin living an honest life without repenting for the lies you've been hiding and asking God—and others—for forgiveness.

You probably dealt with many of your lies in the repentance and forgiveness chapters, but if not, now is the time to work through them. Start with any kind of secret life. Confess your ongoing sin and deceitfulness to the Lord, and ask him for forgiveness. Remember that this is not a moment of shame or tension between you and God—it's a beautiful reunion after time apart. He's delighted that you are taking steps toward him, and he is ready and happy to forgive. Then, do whatever you need to do to interrupt that pattern and put a stop to the secret life. Once the big stuff is out of the way, get right with God on the smaller dishonesties, and let the Holy Spirit lead you in dealing with past lies.

Personal Action

If you have a secret life you are covering up, confess it to the Lord and ask for forgiveness.

Now, make an accountability plan for dealing with that secret life. Who are you going to tell, and when?

What stopgaps can you put in place to help you avoid falling back into the same pattern?

If you make a mistake, what commitment will you make in advance to get yourself back to living honestly?

Next, consider smaller dishonesties in your past. Ask God to help you remember the lies you need to confess to him. Make a list of these, then ask forgiveness for each one.

Finally, ask the Holy Spirit whether you need to follow up with someone else about any of those past lies. Do your best to be open and listen for the Holy Spirit. (Remember, it often feels like a twist or a pull in your conscience.) Write down anyone you need to confess a lie to, and make a plan to follow through.

PARENTING TIP

Help your children preplan good decisions so they aren't tempted to lie to you about their behavior. For example, teach them how to politely say no when friends invite them to watch a show that isn't allowed in your home.

Next, we have to commit to living honestly as we move forward in our lives. First and foremost, this begins with a commitment to live in a way that doesn't need covering up. It means choosing not to gossip, not to spend money we wouldn't want our spouse to know about, not to indulge when no one else is around.

It means working a little harder in order to meet our boss's expectations. It means taking the trash bin out to the street instead of pretending to forget so your husband has to do it.

Now, none of us can possibly be perfect. As humans, we can't *not* sin. We will continue to sin for the rest of our lives, and every time we do we'll be tempted to cover it up with deceit. Therefore, the second piece of this commitment to an honest life is a commitment to choose honesty over deceit when you make a mistake.

For instance, consider the time I made a commitment to stop gossiping. Inevitably, I messed up and gossiped about the dance team captain at my children's school. Instead of sweeping it under the rug and saying I'd get it right next time, I confessed my sin and apologized to her the next time I saw her. And you know what? I was a lot better at not gossiping after that, because I never wanted to have that kind of conversation again.

Whenever possible, repent of your deceit immediately—even right in the middle of telling a lie. Accept the consequences, and move forward with the peace and protection of the Lord. It's a lot easier to toss bricks aside before the mortar dries.

Personal Reflection

What kind of small lies do you tell on a regular basis?

What changes can you make in your behavior so that you won't feel the need to tell those lies?

Write a statement committing to an honest life before the Lord. Commit to living with integrity and coming clean when you don't.

The Lord delights when we live like the people we were created to be. People of integrity receive rich reward through peace, comfort, and relationship. By cultivating an honest life, you are opening your heart to God's wisdom and setting yourself free from a life looking over your shoulder. You can have faith that your integrity will spill over into your spouse, your children, your friends, and your family. Remember that even when you make mistakes, the Lord is always extending an open and loving hand to you. Living an honest life is not about earning his love—it's about removing the walls you've built that prevent you from truly experiencing his love for you, which is always unconditional.

Rocket Prayer

"Lord, give me self-control so I can live an honest life."

Pray this prayer when you are tempted to sin. Pray this prayer when you have sinned and are tempted to cover it up. You cannot possibly live an honest life on your own, so build a habit of inviting God to help you—especially in moments of decision-making.

Prayer of Response

Before you close this workbook for the rest of the week, take a few minutes to write a prayer of response to God. First, thank him for ways he has been good to you. Then, tell him what you're thinking and feeling as you process what you've learned.

Pass It On

Consider passing on what you've learned this week by taking your children's dishonesty seriously, even when it seems funny or harmless. Kids learn early that lying is a great way to get what they want or avoid consequences.

When you catch your child sinning, give him an opportunity to repent right away instead of resorting to deceit. For example, let's say you notice your son cheating at a board game you're playing as a family. Gently ask him if you could speak to him privately, and lovingly confront him about his sin. Your side of the conversation might look like this: "Hey, I noticed that you're not playing this game in a fair way. Don't lie to me to cover it up. I saw you, and I've seen you do it when we've played this game before. I'm not angry with you. I know you really like winning, but it's never OK to be dishonest in order to get what you want. What do you think you need to do to make it right? Yes, I think moving your piece back is a great idea. And what do you need to say to your brother? You do that when we go back in there, and we can keep playing, OK?"

When your child lies to cover up a sin she's already committed, ensure that she experiences consequences—not only for the bad behavior she tried to cover up, but for the lie she told. For example, let's say your daughter snuck a cookie before dinner, even though she knows you don't allow sweets until after the meal. You notice the Oreo bits in her teeth and ask her about it, and she tells a boldface lie. Start by disciplining her for sneaking a cookie. (You might say her brother gets two cookies after dinner instead of just one because he obeyed and waited.) Then, discipline her for telling a lie—and make sure she knows that the punishment is for the lie, not the original misbehavior. (We will discuss disciplines in a later chapter.) Remind her that she never would have had to face either of those consequences if she had obeyed in the first place.

Another great way to help children live honest lives is to cultivate their self-control. After all, an honest life begins with choosing not to sin in the first place. Try games and exercises at home that challenge your child to exercise self-control. For example, let's say your daughter, Allie, desperately wants to play with a doll that her sister is using. Tell Allie that she can play with the doll in five minutes—but she must have a good attitude while waiting. Set a timer where she can see it. If Allie obeys the rules for those five minutes, give her a turn with the doll.

living generously

*Don't store up treasures here on earth, where moths eat them and rust destroys them,
and where thieves break in and steal. Store your treasures in heaven,
where moths and rust cannot destroy, and thieves do not break in and steal.
Wherever your treasure is, there the desires of your heart will also be.*

MATTHEW 6:19–21

When Don and I were first married, we really struggled to make ends meet. Every month we watched our pennies, but some months we had to juggle bills just to keep the electricity on. One Sunday during this season, our pastor gave a compelling sermon on generosity, and we both felt convicted to make giving a priority despite our circumstances. I remember looking at the numbers, trying to figure out how to make it work. We didn't have any margin at all. "We can't even afford to buy toothpaste," I told Don. "How can we possibly give?" He responded with a bold proposal: "Let's give ten percent first—before our bills—and see what God does." Together, we decided to take this next step of faith and obedience to the Lord. It was scary for me—I liked food and electricity, and I knew we'd end up going without one or the other if God didn't show up.

Personal Reflection

What emotions do you feel when you think about your current financial situation? Anxiety? Guilt? Gratitude?

Rank the following in order of priority in your life: saving, spending, and giving. (Spending includes covering necessities like mortgage and utility bills.) Be honest. This isn't about your ideals—it's about how you actually live.

For most of us, spending comes first. In deciding how to use our money, we start by taking care of all the basics: rent or mortgage, utility bills, insurance, food, diapers, and so on. Some of us then stop to set aside a savings goal, while others jump straight to discretionary spending—Netflix, restaurant meals, cut and color—and simply save what's left. Regardless, it's safe to say that giving generally comes last, if at all. When deciding how much to give away (or whether to give at all), the question is usually: "What's left?"

God calls us to view our money very differently. In fact, Scripture makes clear that our money is not truly ours at all. It is God's, and we are simply stewards—trusted to handle the money according to God's priorities, not our own.

Personal Reflection

Read Luke 19:12–24.

What was the top priority for the two servants the master was pleased with?

Describe what kind of servant you have been with the money God has entrusted to you.

Spend a few minutes talking to the Lord. If you've had an ungodly attitude about the money entrusted to you, confess that, and ask for the Lord's forgiveness. Ask him to help you believe that his vision for the way you use your money is for your benefit—not some kind of burdensome tax.

That very first month Don and I gave 10 percent of our income to the church before paying any bills, God worked a miracle. At the end of the month, we somehow had enough to pay every bill, even though no extra money came in. We even had enough for toothpaste! I don't know how he did it. That month, and in the months that followed, we experienced the truth that God is faithful to those who obey him, and God's faithfulness began to change our perspective on money. It turns out that money wasn't the foundation to stand on—it wasn't what would provide the things we wanted and needed. God was.

Personal Reflection

How do you feel about the idea of giving before you spend?

What are you afraid you'd have to give up?

If the idea of giving before you spend or save elicits anxiety in you, you're far from alone. Many of us feel we do not have enough to be generous. Between managing our homes, providing for our children, and saving for college funds, it just seems reckless. We see giving first as the luxury of millionaires who don't have to worry about having enough left over.

But here's the thing: if you live in America and have Wi-Fi in your home, you are among the wealthiest people in the world. You aren't just doing OK. You are filthy rich—even when you take into account the cost of living in the States.

So why don't we feel rich? Well, for starters, our materialistic culture leads us to spend all that wealth on things we don't need. We buy the designer purse because the seventy-percent-off sale was too good to pass up. We buy the bookshelf (and decorative items to fill it) simply to cover empty wall space. This is also true on a larger scale. Instead of buying a modest home with just enough space for our family, we buy the biggest and nicest house we can. Instead of being happy with a car that gets us safely from one place to the next, we buy the fanciest vehicle our budget will allow. When making spending decisions, big or small, we're more likely to ask "What can we afford?" than "What do we really need?"

The result, of course, is that we stretch our incomes thin and even go into debt—all for the sake of luxuries. At the same time, we're constantly exposed to the things we don't have. Advertising is all around us, and we watch television shows, read magazines, and follow Instagram stars that reveal the lifestyles of the rich and famous.

Altogether, this creates an inaccurate sense of poverty—and I'm as guilty as anyone. For me, things really began to change when I met a pastor named Esperito in Uganda. Esperito lived in a small hut with a dirt floor, no electricity, and no toilet. He didn't even have a door. He ate one meal a day—food most of us would refuse, but that he felt grateful for. Any one of us would describe him as destitute. Yet Esperito fasted one day each week and gave the money he saved to widows and orphans who had even less than he did.

When he shared this, I was overcome with shame. How could I possibly feel like I didn't have enough? How could we live in such a big house and give so little? Esperito didn't just give away extra or cut back on luxuries to support others. He made real sacrifices each week in order to love others with Christ-like generosity. Clearly, I had some learning to do.

Personal Reflection

Spend a few minutes doing some uncomfortable self-evaluation. What feelings do you have right now?

When deciding how to spend your money, do you think about what you really need or about what you can afford?

Name a few ways you spend money on selfish desires.

The point of all this isn't to make you feel guilty or to make you give out of shame or obligation, but to guide you in embracing God's perspective on money. We have been believing lies: *It's my money. I deserve this new dress. I need a bigger kitchen. I need to look my best.* All of these "I" thoughts are focused on self-gratification. They convey an indifference to the majority of people in the world who have so little—people the Lord loves just as much as he loves us. They convey that we think our personal priorities are more important than God's. Hebrews 13:16 says, "Don't forget to do good and to share with those in need. These are the sacrifices that please God." In order to make change, we have to recognize just how far off we've been. Taking a hard look in the mirror can sting.

It's also important to note that there's nothing inherently wrong with owning a nice home, taking a Caribbean cruise, or spending a pretty penny on spa visits. What matters is our heart's priorities.

Consider my dear friends John and Karen. Many years ago, this couple made a bold commitment to generosity: starting at 10 percent, they promised to increase their giving by 1 percent each year. When they began, John and Karen worked hard and lived modestly. Now, they own a lake home and take regular vacations around the world—even though they now give away more than half their income. Is it sinful for John and Karen to spend money on luxuries? No! They have faithfully stewarded God's money by making immense generosity their top priority. The Lord has blessed them with wealth, and he delights to see them enjoy it.

Personal Reflection

Look back at Luke 19:12–24. Consider the first servant, who invested the money and doubled it. What was his reward?

The last servant didn't invest the money, but he did keep it safe—something we might consider wise. What did the master say to him? What implications does this have for those of us who prefer caution and security?

Read Matthew 6:19–21, and rewrite the last sentence below.

Where we put our money, our heart follows. This means we must make generosity intentional and consistent. Random acts of kindness are wonderful additions, but the Luke parable shows us that God desires wise and intentional investment. It also tells us that when we invest his money his way, he will provide for us and entrust us with more.

For most of us, switching to this kind of giving-first lifestyle is going to require serious change—and a serious conversation with our families. There are a few basic principles to keep in mind.

First, make this conversation an invitation—not a confrontation. You want your husband and family to join you on this journey. Stay focused on the vision. Explain how giving first reprioritizes our hearts and brings our perspective in line with the Lord. Read the parable in Luke together, and talk about the implications. (The story of the widow's offering in Mark 12:41–44 is also relevant.) Remember that our ultimate goal is to honor God by stewarding his money his way, not to save money or adopt a trendy, minimalistic lifestyle.

Second, be realistic about the hardships. Talk with your family about the changes you'll have to make in your spending. But also talk about how these changes provide opportunities for God to come through and surprise you with blessings. Encourage them to watch and see what God does.

Third, if your husband is on board, collaborate and dream with him about how to give. Pick a percentage together, and look into ministries you're both excited about. Invite your kids to share their input, and have conversations about how everyone in the family can cut back on spending. If your husband is not willing to make changes as a family, remember that you can still be generous as an individual. Even if you can't commit to giving a percentage of your household income, you can commit to giving some of the money you are responsible for. Let him know that you intend to make generosity your personal priority, and explain that you'll carve out money to give away by cutting back on your own personal spending. Who knows, the Lord may use your faithfulness to change your husband's heart later.

Personal Reflection

What do you see as roadblocks to living a giving-first life? (For example, you may be in debt or addicted to shopping.)

What practical steps can you take to remove these roadblocks? (For example, you might sign up for a class to help you get out of debt.)

Make a plan on how to move forward with these steps in the next week.

So, how do you get started? The first step is to focus on shifting your mindset to a genuine giving-first mentality. Remember, the goal is not simply to give. It's to steward God's money God's way. The question is not "How much can I afford to give?" or "How do I get out of debt so I can consider giving?" The question is: "How can I reorder my life in order to give first?" Just like Don and I trusted that God would provide money for food and electricity, you are called to trust that the Lord will provide for your needs.

The next step is to make a plan for giving. We'll talk about how to adjust your spending later, but we must remember that giving comes first.

Personal Reflection

Take a few minutes to pray. Open your heart to the Lord and release any resistance to him. Confess your fears, and ask for his peace and joy.

If your husband is on board with this change, pray together about the percentage of your income the Lord wants you to start giving. Write it down here.

If your husband is not on board with this change, ask that the Lord would soften his heart. Then, pray about what personal spending the Lord would like you to sacrifice in order to give. Write it down here.

Pray about how the Lord wants you to distribute your giving. What is he calling you to give to your church? Are there other ministries, families, or missionaries he's asking you to support?

Write a commitment to giving even when things are tight. Remember he wants us to give sacrificially, like Esperito.

Next, you need to make some practical changes to your budget. Now that you've committed to giving first, you likely need to curb your spending habits.

Personal Action

Make a detailed budget spreadsheet, if you don't already have one. (You can also use a digital budgeting service, if you prefer.) Include your giving commitment, savings goals, and set bills, such as mortgage and car payments, utilities, etc.

How much do you have left over for discretionary spending?

If you need to tweak your spending habits, start with changes to your personal spending. Here are some ideas:

- Learn to make good coffee at home instead of paying daily visits to a coffee shop.
- Switch to a hairstyle that lasts longer between visits. For instance, you might opt for an ombre style that doesn't need regular root touchups.
- Groom the dog yourself.
- Cut back on shopping for clothes and accessories. (How many pairs of jeans do you really need, anyway?)
- Pack your lunch for work. To make this easier, cook a big batch of something over the weekend so you don't have to assemble a new meal every day.
- Cut back on beauty spending, such as eliminating expensive fake eyelashes. (This is probably a healthy challenge to your vanity, too.)
- Invite friends to your home instead of going out for drinks.
- Use cloth diapers (and wash them yourself) instead of disposables.

Personal Reflection

What are you personally going to change in order to spend less?

Once you've curbed your own personal spending, consider changes to spending habits that affect the whole family. Here are some ideas:

- Give up cable, satellite TV, or streaming services. These not only cost money, but they suck up your time in an unhealthy way.
- Make eating out a special treat instead of a regular habit. To ease the burden of cooking, invite your husband and children to help you in the kitchen. You'll bond, and they'll learn practical skills.
- Curb your grocery bill. You can find a ton of resources online to help you feed your family for less.
- Identify cheaper (or free) entertainment. For instance, you might opt to go for a hike instead of going to the zoo.

Personal Reflection

What is your family going to change in order to spend less?

Finally, consider whether your bills are truly essential. Yes, you have to pay your car payment or you'll get into trouble. But do you need that fancy minivan with TV screens in the headrests, or would a simpler van work just as well? And what about your mortgage? Could God be calling you to sell your big house and downsize? Making changes in these areas is incredibly challenging—especially in our culture—but God calls us to a pretty radical life. Remember that your value has nothing to do with how others perceive you or your wealth.

Personal Reflection

Spend some time in prayer. Ask the Lord if he is calling you to make big changes.

If you feel the answer is yes, write that change here. Then, make a plan to move forward.

PARENTING TIP

Encourage your children to notice and care about those in need. Help them understand the importance of showing empathy and following through with real help, whether financial or otherwise.

In my own life, I have discovered great joy in generosity. It seems counterintuitive, but it's true. When we've cut back on our own spending and focused on giving away our money and our time, Don and I have found our life filled with energy, rich relationship, and satisfaction. Much to my surprise, the Lord has even gifted me with random things I wanted but chose not to buy. You see, that's part of the beauty of living generously: it makes you blessable. By choosing to deny yourself in order to bless others, you leave room for the Lord to bless you in unexpected ways.

I've also found great joy in living generously beyond our financial giving. After all, money isn't the only thing you have to steward. You also have time (which is the Lord's) and skills (given to you by God so you can bless others). You also have a lot of possessions you probably don't need. As you reorder your life in order to give first, consider how the Lord might be calling you to invest these other resources, too. Here are some ideas:

- Volunteer at church or with a local nonprofit.
- Give hospitality by inviting neighbors to your home, asking the new family at church to join you on a camping trip, or opening your home to someone who is getting back on her feet after a divorce.
- Donate things you don't need to a refugee family. Call a local agency that works with refugees, and they'll put you in touch with a family that's new to your city and in need. Invite your friends and family to contribute, too.
- Have a garage sale. Clean out all the stuff your family doesn't need, and give away the proceeds.

Personally, my favorite way to give is what I call "double helping." If you're willing to get creative, there are so many ways to be generous in more than one way at a time. Here are two ideas based on my own experience:

- The next time you attend a fundraising auction for your kids' school, give your bid money to a single mom. Tell her to use the money to bid on something for herself. Not only does the school benefit from the bid, but that mom feels loved and gets to pick out an unexpected gift.

- Organize a clothing swap. Suggest that each participant put $10 into a donation jar, but keep everything else free. Make it extra fun by providing lemonade or snacks. When it's over, donate the unwanted clothing to a local nonprofit and give the cash donations to a cause of your choice. Not only do ministries benefit from the clothes and the cash, but participants get to clean out their closets and take home new clothes for free.

Personal Reflection

What skills has God given you?

Name at least three specific ways you could use those skills to benefit others.

Were you inspired by any of the examples above? Make a list of ways you'd like to live generously beyond your giving commitment.

When we make a commitment to living generously, we make a commitment to living more like Jesus. It's not about checking a box or avoiding eternal punishment—it's about living the way God designed us to live, which turns out to be wonderfully freeing and fulfilling. The amazing reality is that when we give ourselves away, that's when we truly find ourselves. The Message translation does a great job of capturing this in Matthew 16:25–26: "Self-sacrifice is the way, my way, to finding yourself, your true self. What kind of deal is it to get everything you want but lose yourself?"

I'm reminded of a quote by Jim Elliott my dad taught me as a child: "He is no fool who gives what he cannot keep to gain what he cannot lose." We cannot keep our money. We cannot keep our beauty. We cannot keep our stuff. But we can keep Jesus and his ever-expanding kingdom. This is what living generously is all about: giving away the stuff we cannot keep in order to gain what the world can never take from us.

Rocket Prayer

"Lord, I put you on the throne of my finances."

Say this prayer when you feel anxious about your finances. Say this prayer when you want to spend money on something you shouldn't. Your money isn't really yours at all, so get into the practice of inviting God into your spending decisions.

Prayer of Response

Before you close this workbook for the rest of the week, take a few minutes to write a prayer of response to God. First, thank him for ways he has been good to you. Then, tell him what you're thinking and feeling as you process what you've learned.

Pass It On

Whenever possible, let your children be the representatives of family giving. For example, give them cash each Sunday to put in the offering basket. Or, let them be the ones to hand a box of food to the family begging outside the grocery store. Also look for opportunities to volunteer as a whole family, such as doing yardwork for an elderly neighbor.

If your child expresses compassion for someone else or has an idea to give generously, pay attention and engage—even if the timing isn't convenient for you. For example, if your daughter notices that a boy in her class doesn't have a coat (or has a really ratty one), talk about how she could help. Does she have some money she could put toward buying a coat for the boy? Does her big brother have a coat he's outgrown?

Finally, consider teaching your children the concepts of giving, saving, and spending by helping them organize their allowance and birthday money into three different jars. Read relevant Scripture together, and talk about why giving needs to come first.

PARENTING A NEW WAY

THREE WEEKS

In this final section, we narrow our focus specifically onto parenting choices, exploring how standing on God allows us to parent with long-term purposefulness.

Note: As these chapters are focused entirely on how we engage with our children, they will not include Pass It On sections.

15

empowering your children

We can rejoice, too,
when we run into problems and trials,
for we know that they help us develop endurance.

ROMANS 5:3

When my friend Kim's daughter Abbey was about eight years old, she asked to take horseback riding lessons. At the very first lesson, Kim watched as her excited daughter climbed up on a horse for the very first time—then got snapped at by the instructor for not being able to make the horse move forward. To Kim's surprise, the instructor continued to yell at Abbey with an unreasonably harsh tone. It wasn't the tough love of a coach—it was downright unprofessional and abrasive.

Naturally, Kim's instincts told her to intervene. She wanted to hop the fence and give that instructor a piece of her mind. She wanted to file a complaint with the woman's boss. But something in her spirit held her back. This was an opportunity to teach Abbey how to respond when she was treated unjustly—a valuable life lesson. Besides, as long as she stayed close by, Abbey was not in any danger. So, she held her tongue.

Personal Reflection

Describe a time when you thought your child was being treated unfairly. How did you respond?

After the lesson, Kim talked with Abbey about what had happened. "Sometimes people don't treat us the way they should," she told her daughter, "and God still wants us to respond to them in a way that pleases him. You don't need to be afraid, because I'll be there with you at each lesson if you want to go back." Then, they prayed together about the situation, and even prayed for the instructor. Surprisingly, Abbey was ready to go back for another lesson the next week.

When they arrived for the second lesson, the owner of the barn met them and said, "I will be Abbey's teacher. Your instructor is no longer employed here." Apparently, another mother had seen how the instructor treated Abbey and reported it. The owner did a great job as an instructor, and Abbey had a wonderful summer of riding.

Now, some of you might be horrified by the way Kim handled the situation. You might think she failed Abbey by not fighting back against unfair treatment. But you know what Abbey learned from that experience? She learned how to respond graciously—like a grape, instead of a marble—to injustice. She learned to take her concerns to the Lord instead of acting on impulse. And more important, she learned that God comes through and provides for his children when they turn to him.

Personal Reflection

How do you feel about the idea of allowing your children to experience pain and unfairness?

Describe a time when you endured a season of hardship. What did you learn from that experience?

When, as moms, should we protect our kids from hardship? When should we allow them to experience pain? As parents, this an incredibly challenging dance.

Most of us err on the side of being Mama Bear. There's a reason "helicopter parenting" is a common phrase in our culture. We intervene when our kids get into an argument. We yell at the coach for putting our child on the bench. We fight back against punishments at school. I've even heard of mothers attending job interviews with their grown children—then calling the company to argue when their children didn't get the job. Yikes!

Personal Reflection

Describe a time in your own life when you faced hard consequences after making a bad decision.

What lesson did you learn from that experience?

Of course, we act like Mama Bear because we love our children. We remember the days of feeding them, snuggling with them, and changing their diapers. We want to create a world for them where they can play and learn and work without fear or failure. We hate the idea of seeing them suffer.

But here's the reality: protecting our children from pain at every turn does not prepare them for adulthood. In fact, it can seriously hurt their chances at living responsible, stable, and healthy lives. It can even hinder their own relationships with the Lord. You see, when you overprotect your children, they learn one thing: that they need mom. Not that they need God. Not that they are capable of working harder, of navigating conflict, of overcoming a setback. And while some of us might love the idea of being needed by our sweet children forever, we must remember this: they are the King's children, we are their nannies, and our job is to raise them for effective service to the kingdom.

So, what then? Do we turn a blind eye when our children are about to make bad decisions? Do we ignore the situation when a bully or an authority figure treats our child unfairly? Do we remove boundaries that protect them from dangerous people or inappropriate media? Of course not. The goal isn't to leave them to their own devices. The goal is to empower them to make wise choices on their own, learn from life's hard lessons, build perseverance, and respond in a godly way to all kinds of circumstances. By coming alongside our children with guidance and encouragement in teachable moments, we can help them grow up to live healthy lives. It's about the big picture, not the immediate circumstances.

Personal Reflection

Read James 1:2–4. What kind of attitude does the Lord want us to have in our difficult circumstances?

Take a moment to pray. Thank the Lord for the trials in your own life that have produced perseverance. Write down your thoughts.

One of the hardest things about parenting this way is that it requires us to let go of the arrogant idea that we can save our children. Think about it: being Mama Bear might seem selfless on the surface, but really it reflects an inherent belief that you alone know what's right for your kid—not anyone else, not even God. By trying to maintain control, you're suggesting that you're the only one who deserves control—and that just isn't true. Our children are capable. Other adults have great insights. And God knows far better than you what's going on in your child's heart.

That last one is important. Being a Foundational Parent ultimately means trusting that God is the only one who can truly comfort your child, protect your child, guide your child, and lead your child to a fulfilling and thriving life. Not you.

Accepting this and living like it's true means surrendering our pride. We have to let go of the idea that we can save our kids. We also have to let go of what others think about us. We can't allow ourselves to jump up and intervene on our child's behalf simply because other parents might think we're not trying hard enough if we don't. After all, God is the best parent, and he frequently chooses to remain quiet. He offers comfort and wisdom when we seek it, but he doesn't always rescue us from pain—even though it hurts him to see us hurting. He allows us to experience the consequences of our actions, and he allows us to endure hardships that feel random and unfair. We can take a page out of his parenting book by resisting the urge to constantly rescue our children— even if others disapprove. Sacrificing our own reputation is the truly selfless choice.

Personal Reflection

Spend a few minutes reflecting. Describe a time you intervened to shield your child for reasons that were ultimately selfish. (For instance, perhaps you were worried about your own reputation or you thought it was easier to fix the situation yourself than help your child navigate it.)

Ultimately, parenting in this way is about posture. Mama Bear parenting looks like looming over your children and holding them tightly to yourself. A Mama Bear's eyes are fierce and constantly on the lookout for danger. Her mouth is ready to bite and her claws are ready to fight. Foundational Parenting looks like gently holding your children up to God with an open heart and open hands. A Foundational mom's eyes are looking upward at Christ, and her mouth is closed as she listens to him.

Personal Reflection

What fears do you have about surrendering to God's parenting plan for your children?

You might be thinking, *That sounds like a nice concept, but what does it look like in reality?* Fair question. As I said earlier, this is an incredibly challenging dance. In the remainder of this chapter, we'll explore a few practical areas where many of us feel the need to intervene and protect our kids.

Let's start by considering legitimately dangerous situations, such as when our children run into busy streets, reach for a hot stove, or encounter seriously sketchy strangers. In these situations, our Mama Bear instincts are good. By all means, please intervene, no matter how old your children are. The trick is to have a thoughtful conversation with your child after the danger has passed. If the big picture goal is to empower our children to make wise choices on their own, it's important that they understand why you responded the way you did. Once you've gotten your own emotion under control, talk about the situation so your child can learn good safety rules.

If the dangerous situation involved a person or place that was dangerous, you'll need to have an age-appropriate and nuanced conversation with your child about how they can handle future situations, especially if you're not there to intervene. After all, it's pretty easy to learn not to touch a hot stove, but it's not so easy to learn how to recognize whether a stranger is safe or dangerous. I recommend looking for resources about this in other books and online. For instance, the "Tricky People" approach might be more empowering for your kids than the traditional "Stranger Danger" motto.

Personal Reflection

Name a few external dangers your children might realistically face in the near future.

Take a moment to pray. Ask the Lord how you should handle those situations, then write about how you're going to use them as teachable moments.

Next, let's consider exposure to inappropriate things. This includes media (such as movies, music, television shows, and websites), as well as things they might see or hear in real life. This category presents a more subtle danger, as these things affect our children internally through their mind and heart.

First, I encourage you to take these things seriously. Images and ideas sink in. It is crucial to set healthy boundaries and monitor these things—especially when our children are young. It's OK to be Mama Bear and shield your children as best you can in the early years. Use parental controls and be picky about which other children and adults they spend time with.

As our children get older, we have to slowly shift from shielding to empowering. After all, your children won't be living at home forever. Create a culture in your home of having open conversations about the images, ideas, and language they encounter. When they ask why they can't watch a certain movie or listen to certain music, don't simply say, "you're not old enough." Find an age-appropriate way to provide a real and transparent answer. For instance, when your fourth-grader asks why he can't listen to a song that sexualizes women, you might say, "That song might have a great beat, but the lyrics are really disrespectful to girls. Our culture sometimes treats girls like their appearance is the only thing that matters, instead of their brains or their hearts. In our family, we don't support that or pretend it's OK." This approach helps prepare them to evaluate and make wise choices in middle school, high school, college, and beyond.

As best you can, steer your kids toward friends who exhibit obedience, honesty, and respectfulness. If your child befriends a neighbor or classmate whose home is a less-than-ideal environment, set some boundaries. For example, you might say no to playdates at the friend's home but welcome him into your house as long as he abides by your family's rules. It can be really hard to walk the line between doing what's best for your child and loving your neighbors, so talk to your mentor about any challenging situations.

As your children approach middle school, continue to use smart parental controls to prevent exposure to violent and sexual images, and set boundaries around media and technology. At the same time, don't keep them completely withdrawn from culture. Talk about the things they're curious about, including other religions and social beliefs. It's good for them to know that other people have different beliefs, and it's crucial that they have guidance on how to navigate those differences. Cultivating a culture of conversation in your family means your kids are more likely to come to you with questions rather than simply turn to their friends or the internet.

Personal Reflection

What inappropriate things are your children exposed to in this season of life?

Take those things to the Lord in prayer. Ask him how you are to go forward in the future.

Are there any boundaries you need to adjust?

How can you turn this exposure into a teaching moment?

Next, let's consider conflict with others. Whether it's an argument with a sibling or tension with a teacher, we're often quick to simply handle the situation ourselves. In this arena, most of us need to take a big step toward empowering instead of shielding—even if our children are quite young.

When your child experiences conflict with someone else, think of yourself as a coach instead of a manager. For example, let's say your daughter comes running upstairs, claiming that her brother won't share a toy. Instead of yelling a command to your son, advise your daughter on how to handle the situation herself. Start by helping her consider what role she might have in the conflict. After all, it takes two to tango. Even if she's only responsible for 1 percent of the problem at hand, learning to reflect and recognize her percent is an amazing life skill that will improve her future relationships. Then, use guiding questions to help her come up with healthy ways to handle the problem. Pray together about her emotions before she goes back downstairs. This way, she learns to recognize her feelings and take them to the Lord instead of being controlled by them.

The situation is tougher when the conflict involves another adult, such as a teacher or a coach, but often the same four basic principles apply. We want to coach our children to:

- Accurately assess their role in the conflict
- Identify and deal with their emotions
- Take it to the Lord
- Come up with wise responses to the problem

For example, let's say your son has a tense relationship with his teacher. She tends to treat him with exasperation because he talks a lot during class and distracts other students. If your son complains that his teacher doesn't like him, you might help him see his role in the tension, acknowledge how he is feeling, pray about it, and come up with a plan. (For instance, he might make a card for the teacher apologizing for his behavior and saying he'll try hard to do better—a sweet gesture that's bound to make her think twice about her own attitude.)

Personal Reflection

Describe a few common conflicts that arise between siblings in your home or between your children and their friends.

Describe a time your child had a conflict with an adult.

Take some time to pray and share your concerns with the Lord. Then, make a plan for how you are going to use similar future situations as teachable moments.

Sometimes, our children face conflicts with other adults that cross the line into authority abuse. (Abbey's horseback riding teacher is a great example.) These situations can be very emotionally charged. But when you feel the urge to jump in reactively, stop and pray. Sometimes the Lord instructs us to intervene, but most often he asks us to hold our tempers and let him use the situation in his own way, just like he did with Kim.

When my daughter, Cammy, was a young teen, she had a basketball coach who obviously treated her more harshly than the other players—so much so that other parents commented to me about it. Like Kim, I wanted to intervene as a Mama Bear, but when I prayed about it I felt the Lord asking me to hold back. Instead, I wiped away her tears after each practice and taught her how to process the prejudice and bullying. The mistreatment continued throughout Cammy's season with that coach, and though I never had the satisfaction of seeing the situation completely resolved, I did get glimpses of what the Lord was doing. During that season, several of Cammy's teammates opened up to her about pain in their own lives, and I believe they trusted her because of the way she handled the situation with the coach. Though it was hard to watch her suffer, my daughter matured and grew in her faith during that difficult season—just like I did when I spent a summer surrendering to an unjust boss at summer camp as a teen.

As adults, your children will inevitably face situations where they are treated unfairly, sometimes by bosses, instructors, or other authorities. We won't always be there to rescue them. And so, even though it feels counterintuitive, we give our children a gift when we allow them to endure these seasons of hurt while we're still there to comfort them and help them learn how to respond well.

Of course, these kinds of situations do require quiet vigilance. If the situation were ever to become dangerous, you'd want to know, and you'd want to intervene. Have a conversation with your child about where the line is. Make sure he knows to tell you or another adult immediately if the authority figure ever threatens him, gets physically aggressive, or uses language or contact that's sexual in nature.

Personal Reflection

Describe a time when another adult treated your child in an unjust way. How did you respond?

Take a few minutes to pray about this concept. Give your concerns to God and ask for guidance.

Finally, let's consider situations when your child might face painful consequences for his or her own decisions. Allowing kids to experience the consequences of their actions is really healthy thing, but it can be tough as a parent to put away our Mama Bear instincts.

When my son Blair was a senior in high school, he got drunk on campus during a basketball game. Because a friend saw and called Don, we were able to pick Blair up before he got caught or caused any trouble, which raised an interesting dilemma for us as parents. The school's policy stated that any student who got drunk on campus would be suspended for two weeks—a punishment that could put a stain on his college applications. But at that point, no school officials knew what had happened. We could either inform the school and see our son experience the full cost of his actions, or we could be thankful Blair dodged those serious consequences.

The following Monday, Don went with our son to the principal's office. Per our decision, Blair began confessing what he'd done. The principal quickly interrupted. "Stop!" he said. "If you tell me more, I will have to suspend you." Blair paused, looked to Don for confirmation, and continued. He walked out of the office with a two-week suspension. The principal told us later that the appointment right before ours was a mom whose daughter had also gotten drunk on campus that weekend—and had gotten caught. This woman had yelled at the principal and even threatened a lawsuit if the school suspended her daughter.

That mom was acting on her Mama Bear instincts. She wanted to protect her almost eighteen-year-old daughter from tough consequences. But did her actions really serve her daughter in the long run? I don't think so. Blair made a bad decision, and it was important to us that he learn that bad decisions have real-life consequences beyond punishment from mom and dad.

When our kids are young, the consequences of their actions can seem trivial—so trivial that we decide they don't really matter, and we save our children from stress or pain because we don't want to deal with a tantrum. But it's essential that we allow our young children to experience consequences, even when it's inconvenient for us.

For example, let's say your daughter got mad and stomped on her party favor at a friend's birthday party. Then, of course, she got sad that it was broken and started to cry. It's tempting to just hand over a replacement—especially if the host mom rushes in to offer another one. It's just a cheap toy. But in your child's world, this consequence is big, and it's important that she face it. Talk it through with her, acknowledging her pain while helping her understand that the toy is gone because of a choice she made. Use guiding questions to talk about how she can handle her anger differently in the future.

Personal Reflection

Describe a time when you rescued your child from the natural consequences of his or her actions.

How could you have turned that situation into a teachable moment?

As caretakers, we have a responsibility to protect our children when necessary. But the reality is that protection isn't necessary nearly as often as we think. Instead, it's often better to allow our children to experience discomfort or engage with a challenging concept. After all, childhood is the training ground for adulthood. Now is the time that they learn how to avoid danger, navigate conflict, make decisions about what to expose themselves to, and turn to the Lord as their foundation. As moms, we must loosen our grip and trust God's way of parenting.

Rocket Prayer

"Lord, empower me to empower my child."

Say this prayer when you feel the urge to intervene. Say this prayer when your child comes to you for help. As a parent, you have a responsibility to empower your children, and sometimes that can feel daunting. Never forget that you have a Father who is always ready and willing to empower *you*.

Prayer of Response

Before you close this workbook for the rest of the week, take a few minutes to write a prayer of response to God. First, thank him for ways he has been good to you. Then, tell him what you're thinking and feeling as you process what you've learned.

16

instilling obedience: concepts and boundaries

Children, obey your parents
because you belong to the Lord,
for this is the right thing to do.

EPHESIANS 6:1

When we were young parents starting our own family, I made a point of watching other families closely, looking for clues about how to raise kids. I took note of characteristics I wanted to see in my children, and sometimes I even asked parents how they did it.

Our pastor's family stuck out to me. As their teenagers left for college and grew into adults, each of them remained faithful to the Lord—something that doesn't always happen in Christian families. One Sunday, I approached him and asked, "How do you make sure your children continue to follow the Lord after they leave home?"

He answered, "Teach them to obey you." My confusion must have been obvious. After a pause, he continued. "You must transfer obedience from you to God. If your children don't know how to obey you, how do you expect them to obey an unseen God?"

Personal Reflection

In the weeks that have passed since we studied obedience in chapter 7, how have you grown in obedience to God? Take a few minutes to journal about this.

I was struck by his answer. How *do* we expect our children to obey an unseen God if they don't obey their parents? Of course their obedience to him is related to their obedience to us.

When we do a good job teaching our children genuine obedience, we instill them with a vital tool they need to hear and respond to their heavenly Father. To explain further, let's look at a conversation I had with our daughter, Cammy, when she was thirteen. She had asked to do something with her friends that she knew we would not agree to. I talked with her about the reasons for my decision, but Cammy said, "Mom, why can't I just do what I want to do? All the other kids get to."

Here's what I told her: "Imagine that when you were born there were hundreds of wires attaching Baby Cammy to Mom. Each of those wires represents something you need to learn. As I see you grow and learn these things, I can unplug those wires from me and plug them into God instead. Eventually, all your wires will plug directly into God. That's my job as a mom: to raise you for a healthy relationship of dependence on God. You are not ready to make good choices and obey God in this area yet. You are asking me to unplug a bunch of wires and throw them to the wind. In other words, you're asking me to be bad at my job. I am watching your character, and you'll be able to do what you want when I can see that you're ready to submit your choices to God."

This wire analogy isn't perfect, but it creates an image of what we're talking about in this chapter: teaching our children to truly obey us so that we can transfer that obedience to God. This is crucial because obedience is an absolutely essential aspect of a foundational relationship with the Lord. Obedience to the Lord reflects our trust in him, and it opens the door to deep relationship with him. As nannies to the King's children, we must teach them this healthy obedience.

Personal Reflection

What fears or hesitations do you have about teaching your children to obey?

By healthy obedience, I mean obedience that is complete, immediate, and with a good attitude. (See chapter 7 for a refresher on these concepts.) I'm not simply talking about teaching our children to be compliant, and I'm certainly not talking about stripping children of their voice or their spirit. I'm talking about teaching our children to voluntarily cooperate because they trust us and defer to our decisions—not because they fear our anger or even understand the reasons behind our request. God wants us to obey because we love him and defer to his wisdom. Therefore, it's the kind of obedience we want to teach our children.

Teaching our children obedience is a huge and complicated task, so we're splitting this concept into two chapters. In this chapter, we're going to continue exploring important big-picture principles of obedience and then talk about how to take the first step: setting clear and healthy boundaries for our children. In the next chapter, we'll tackle what to do when our children cross those boundaries—because we all know they will. The way we handle discipline can make or break the lessons our children learn about obedience.

Personal Reflection

Take a moment to assess the status of obedience in your home. Are your children fairly submissive, or do they consistently defy you?

Describe their heart attitude when they defy you.

Name a few areas (such as mealtime or bedtime) where there's tension in your home because of disobedience.

For most moms, one of two big problems gets in the way of teaching godly obedience to their children.

First, many of us lack consistency and follow-through. We might set some loose boundaries for our kids, but when the time comes to enforce them, we let the misbehavior slide. This is common among moms who tend toward Passive Parenting, which we discussed way back in the first chapter. Passive moms are often soft on obedience because they hate conflict or don't feel like they have the energy to follow through with consequences. This kind of passivity can also result from fears regarding boundaries and discipline. For example, a mom who grew up in an abusive household might swing too far in the direction of grace because she's trying to avoid acting like her own parents.

When we don't take obedience seriously, our kids follow suit. They quickly learn there aren't consequences for disobedience, and they come to see boundaries as arbitrary—an attitude they take with them into adulthood. These kids grow up to see rules as empty guidelines that don't have a purpose or come with any consequences—whether those rules come from society, their employer, or God.

The second problem is that those of us who do follow through consistently are often prone to being too harsh, and we instill fear-based obedience instead of submissive obedience. We lose our tempers and impose unreasonable consequences, which means our kids only obey out of fear—not genuinely respectful hearts. This is often the case for moms who tend to slip into Behavioral Parenting. Like Passive moms, their motivations are ultimately about their own comfort. They want their children to obey because it makes life easier or makes them look good.

Fear-based obedience doesn't transfer well. Oftentimes, children who grew up obeying out of fear go rogue once they're out from under mom's thumb. They become reckless and abandon the principles they grew up with. Other times, these children develop a fear-based relationship with the Lord. They might abide by God's rules (and everyone else's) on the outside, but their relationship to God is highly legalistic and based on fear of God's wrath instead of love and trust in his goodness. Even if it looks good from the outside, this is not the kind of obedience God wants from our children.

Personal Reflection

In general, which of these two big-picture problems is more prevalent in your parenting?

Take a moment to write a statement below committing yourself to taking obedience seriously and doing what it takes to teach the right kind of obedience—even if it's uncomfortable for you as a mom.

Next, make a few commitments that are specific to your habits. For example, if you tend to be the worst at following through when you're trying to work from home, you might say, "I will consistently follow through with consequences, even when it means taking a break from my work."

So, what does it look like to teach healthy, submissive obedience to our children? For starters, it means setting clear boundaries. Why? Because without boundaries, there can be no obedience or disobedience. Children have to know where the line is before they can decide whether or not to cross it.

It's worth noting that having healthy boundaries for your children isn't just a means to teach obedience. It's also incredibly valuable in and of itself. Here are a few key benefits:

Boundaries keep kids safe. By setting clear limits around where your children can and can't go or what they can and can't touch, you build metaphorical fences that keep your kids away from danger.

Boundaries help kids feel secure. Too much freedom is overwhelming and confusing. Studies show that having too many options—whether we're choosing a tube of toothpaste or a career path—can be paralyzing for adults. We are actually happier and more confident when we have limitations. The same is even truer for children. When we limit our kids' options, we actually make it easier for them to learn, explore, and cultivate their abilities.

Setting clear boundaries also helps kids feel more secure in their relationship with you. When your children know what you expect from them, your own behavior becomes much less mysterious.

Boundaries prepare kids for the real world. Every environment has some kind of boundary, whether it's a kindergarten classroom or an office where your child lands his first job. These boundaries—some spoken, some unspoken—create order, security, and safety.

By setting boundaries for our children at home, we help them adapt to the reality that they can't move through life doing whatever they please without consequence. This not only makes them more aware of others' needs and perceptions, but helps them accept that there are always rules and expectations at play.

Boundaries help kids learn self-control. In order to comply with your boundaries and avoid discipline, children have to learn how to exercise self-control—a life skill that will serve them well in the long run. Resisting impulses is incredibly challenging for children, whether that impulse is to sneak a cookie before lunch or run around the kitchen during dinnertime. Kids who learn to exercise self-control over these seemingly insignificant impulses are more likely to exercise restraint later in life when hormones are raging and they feel the need for speed.

Personal Reflection

Describe your thoughts and feelings about setting boundaries for your children. Do you do this well? What concerns do you have?

At this point, how do your children handle boundaries?

For many moms, the idea of setting boundaries comes with some hesitation—even if they intellectually agree that boundaries are healthy. Before we dive into the specifics of setting boundaries, let's tackle a few of these:

"I don't want to perpetuate the abusive or harsh upbringing I had." It is wonderful that you want to break this unhealthy cycle in your family! Just remember, one extreme is not necessarily healthier than the other. Loving your children well involves establishing clear boundaries and disciplining in a consistent and compassionate way. Talk to your mentor or a counselor to work through baggage that might be holding you back.

"I did so many bad things when I was young. How can I tell my children not to do them?" Setting boundaries for your children doesn't make you a hypocrite. It makes you someone who learns from her mistakes and uses that wisdom to help others. Wouldn't it be great if they could avoid the same dangers and struggles you experienced? Use your understanding to help them dodge the traps you fell into.

"I want my children to be my friends." As moms, we must play the long game. Right now, our kids need us to be their parents, not their friends. This doesn't mean we have to wait until they're adults to have a deep connection. When our children are young, that deep connection happens through a healthy nurturing and guiding relationship, which includes setting and enforcing boundaries. It's what they need most from us, and without it they will grow to resent us. If we do our jobs well, we can have an adult friendship with our children when they're grown.

"I want my children to be free to be themselves." Somehow as a society we've bought into the idea that any limitations crush a child's spirit, but it's simply not true. Children who grow up with healthy boundaries are more secure and competent than those who had too much freedom, which means they can practice creativity, find their identity, and pursue their dreams with confidence. Kids with good boundaries also know how to use their gifts of boldness, tenacity, and curiosity in healthy ways instead of selfish or destructive ones. The goal of healthy boundaries isn't to quash these spirited qualities, but to cultivate them.

Personal Reflection

Read Exodus 20:1–17. Note that the first three commandments are about how we relate to God, and the rest are about how we relate to people and our world.

If everyone lived by these boundaries, how would our world be different?

From the very beginning, God has shown his extravagant love for humanity by setting boundaries. The first one was simple: you can work six days of the week, but the seventh is for rest. Did this boundary limit Adam and Eve? Yes, but in a way that was wonderfully good for them. It was a gift. Even in the Garden of Eden, humans were given parameters. God knew what boundaries would help us flourish.

Then God set a much more famous one: you can eat from any tree in the garden except one. This, too, was for our benefit. This boundary not only warned Adam and Eve about a very real danger, but it gave them the choice to either submit to God's authority or become judges themselves. This boundary inherently gifted Adam and Eve with freedom, because it made submitting to God's authority a choice.

Of course, we all know what choice they made and what consequences came from it. Out of their choice came the need for many more boundaries: do not kill, do not steal, do not worship any other gods. The book of Leviticus outlines hundreds of boundaries that describe how the Israelites were and were not to conduct themselves. The rules deal with business transactions, gossip, sexual choices, and navigating debt and other legal situations. Again in the New Testament Paul outlines boundaries for the growing community of Christians. In both cases, the rules protect the weakest members of society and forbid actions that would cause pain or unhealthy conflict.

These boundaries were not established to make life easier for God or to needlessly restrict his people as a show of power. They were created because God knows that his people will be happiest and healthiest if they live a certain way. God's boundaries give us the opportunity every day to make the same choice Adam and Eve faced: to defer to God's understanding of right and wrong or to make our own decisions.

The point is this: the very best Father in the world provides boundaries for his children. Those boundaries limit his children, but in doing so sets them free to thrive. We can be confident in taking a page out of his parenting book.

Personal Reflection

Read Exodus 19:5. Consider the "if." Are God's boundaries forced limitations, or are they choices?

What does God promise if we choose to obey his boundaries? (Feel free to draw on verses other than Exodus 19:5. There are many about this!)

What can you learn from God about setting boundaries for your children?

So, we've established that setting healthy boundaries is incredibly beneficial for our children and essential to teaching obedience. But what boundaries are healthy? There are two basic principles that can guide us.

The first is that we should start by providing limited choices to our young children, and then widen the boundaries as they earn more freedom. You can picture this approach like a "V." This empowers our kids to blossom into more freedom as they mature and make good choices. Plus, this approach avoids serious problems in the teenage years. Trust me: if your kids get used to too much freedom early on, they won't be happy when you start reining them in later. We don't want to wait until the stakes are high to start teaching obedience.

Let's consider a practical example that moms of young children deal with every day: what kids wear. When they're babies, we choose their outfits. This is the very bottom of the "V." As they get old enough to have an opinion and learn obedience, we can open up the options—but only a little bit at first. Don't jump straight to allowing your child to put on whatever he wants, even if this means fighting a battle in front of the dresser. Start by allowing the most limited choice, such as which of two shirts he wants to wear. If he throws a fit, stand your ground and choose for him. He must to learn to obey and stay within your boundaries before those boundaries are widened. Only once he consistently complies with a good attitude should you widen the scope.

The second principle is to customize the boundaries to your child. Where you draw the line should depend on her temperament and maturity level. For example, a highly defiant eleven-year-old who likes to start fires should obviously not be allowed to play alone in the barn. At the same time, a younger child with a gentle temperament and good common sense is probably just fine building a hay fort. Think about your child's personality, capabilities, and character, and then draw boundary lines that will benefit her and challenge her to practice respectful submission.

In a household with multiple children, customization is a dance. It is great to have family-wide rules that set shared expectations for everyone, such as telling the truth or putting dishes in the dishwasher after each meal. This is a good way to unify the family and set standards. At the same time, children of different ages and temperaments will need different boundaries when it comes to more specific things. Rest assured that this is OK—even if your children argue that it's unfair.

For instance, let's say you have a boundary in your home that says kids have to finish their homework before they can have screen time. Your daughter loves school and always does her homework quickly and well. Your son, on the other hand, makes up answers to his math problems so it looks like the homework is done. In this case, you need to set an additional boundary for him that a parent must check his homework before he's allowed any screen time. He might argue it's unfair that he has to get his homework checked when his sister doesn't. Instead of giving in and applying an unnecessary boundary to your daughter in the name of equality, explain to your son why the boundaries are where they are. It's healthy for him to see that he can earn more freedom by making better choices.

Personal Reflection

Taking into account each of your children's unique personalities, what boundaries do you think you need to change?

If you have given your children too much freedom, consider how to draw from the "V" principle as you establish new boundaries. Name a few specific boundaries you need to set to help your child learn submission and earn greater freedom.

When you're ready to articulate a boundary to your child, there are three basic steps:

1. State what they can or can't do.
2. If applicable, clearly set timetables and exceptions.
3. Describe the consequences for disobedience.

The goal is to be as clear as possible. We want our children to understand exactly what we expect of them and what consequences they'll experience if they disobey. By clearly stating each of these, we empower our kids to make informed decisions—and we close any loopholes they might use to argue later. Here are a few examples of clear boundary statements:

- "You can play baseball in our yard as long as you don't break anything. If you do, you'll have to stop."
- "You can choose the pink shirt or the purple shirt. If you can't choose, I'll pick for you."
- "You can have a cookie if you eat all your lunch without complaining." (Note: here the consequence is clearly implied, and that's fine. If they complain, they won't get a cookie.)

Notice that these boundaries use positive "you can" statements, even though they ultimately communicate a limitation. Whenever possible, this is more effective than saying "do not" or "you can't" because it keeps kids focused on the fact that they have a choice. You can also phrase boundaries as "if" statements, such as, "If you choose to throw food on the floor, your lunch will be taken away and you'll have to wait until dinner for more." There might not be a "you can" involved here, but the phrasing still keeps kids focused on their power to choose. By framing boundaries this way, our kids learn to think through their actions ahead of time and realize they have a choice and it comes with consequences.

Set boundaries in advance whenever possible. Headed to the park? Go ahead and make some clear boundary statements on the way there. Often, we don't realize the need for a boundary until something goes wrong. That's OK. The trick is to respond to those situations by clearly articulating the new boundary—not punishing the child for something he didn't know was wrong. For instance, let's say you discover your son squirting sunscreen all over the couch. You might be tempted to jump straight to discipline—something we'll cover next week. But if you had never told your son not to squirt sunscreen on the couch, it isn't just to punish him for that behavior. Take a breath, and state the new boundary: "You can squirt the sunscreen onto your body and rub it in, but you cannot squirt it anywhere else. If you do, you will have a timeout."

Next week, as we discuss discipline, we'll address what kind of consequences to put in place as you set boundaries.

Personal Reflection

Practice writing a few clear boundary statements that are relevant to your children. It's OK to leave off the consequences piece for now. We'll follow up with that next week.

Rocket Prayer

"Lord, help me know where to draw the line."

Say this prayer when there's conflict in your home and you need to set a new boundary. Say this prayer when you're afraid your child won't like what you have to say. Remember that the Lord has wisely drawn lines for us because he loves us, and he can help us do the same for our children.

Prayer of Response

Before you close this workbook for the rest of the week, take a few minutes to write a prayer of response to God. First, thank him for ways he has been good to you. Then, tell him what you're thinking and feeling as you process what you've learned.

instilling obedience: navigating discipline

Discipline your children,
and they will give you peace of mind
and will make your heart glad.

PROVERBS 29:17

My friend Sharon grew up in a home with what she generously describes as "difficult family dynamics." Her father, a heavy drinker who didn't spend much time at home, was verbally and physically abusive. At the smallest infraction—and sometimes for no apparent reason at all—he would yell hateful words at Sharon and her sister and lash out at them with violent beatings. Life when he was around was cruel and unpredictable.

In an attempt to compensate for their father's brutality, Sharon's mom gave the girls complete freedom. She set no boundaries and enforced no discipline. She didn't seem to care what Sharon did, whether she was a five-year-old roaming the family ranch or a teenager staying out late. Instead of making Sharon feel safe and supported, the lack of boundaries and discipline left her feeling insecure, unloved, and unmoored with no foundation to stand on.

Personal Reflection

How would you describe your parents' approach to boundaries and discipline?

When Sharon became a parent, she longed to set healthy boundaries for her children, but she had no idea how to enforce them. Her father's violence obviously wasn't the right choice, but her mother's complete nonchalance wasn't much healthier.

Discipline is a challenging topic. Too many of us, like Sharon, have experienced deeply unhealthy disciplinary styles at one end of the spectrum or the other—sometimes both in the same household. These experiences, combined with our era of heightened cultural sensitivity, make it incredibly challenging to know what is and isn't appropriate. Yet discipline is absolutely key to teaching our children healthy, submissive obedience. We simply cannot teach obedience without it.

In the last chapter, we laid the groundwork for why obedience matters and covered the first step to teaching it: setting clear boundaries. This chapter is dedicated to the next step: enforcing those boundaries with compassionate discipline.

Personal Reflection

Read Hebrews 12:5–7 and take a moment to meditate on the words.

Describe a time the Lord disciplined you. How did it bring you into deeper relationship?

Discipline is ultimately about compassion, as counterintuitive as that may seem. When it's done well, discipline isn't about releasing our anger or maintaining order in the house. It's a tool for teaching obedience, which we've already established is essential if we're going to do our job as nannies to the King's children. It's compassionate because it's for their own good. Without it, they won't learn that their actions have consequences, won't learn how to exercise self-control, won't learn the beauty of submitting obediently to God.

Our God is a God of both love and discipline. Over and over again in Scripture, we see God enforce consequences for his people. He sends storms and whales. He sends Babylonian soldiers. These measures felt painful to God's people in the moment, but of course we know how the stories play out—how God used discipline for their good in the long run. As moms, this is the kind of discipline we are called to: discipline that is just, that is strategic, and that is, above all else, out of love.

Personal Reflection

What concerns do you have about disciplining your children?

Is there anything about discipline that makes you uncomfortable?

Discipline is emotionally challenging, even if we ultimately know that it's good. Before we dive into the particulars of healthy discipline, let's tackle a few major concerns that might be getting in your way:

"I know I have anger issues, and I feel like I could easily cross a line." First of all, it is really good that you're self-aware enough to identify this risk in yourself. That said, avoiding discipline altogether is not the answer. In order to love your children well, you need to deal with those anger issues so you can discipline effectively and calmly. Talk to your mentor or a counselor this week about first steps.

"I'm afraid my children will hate me." This was said in the last chapter, but it deserves to be said again: right now, your children need you to be their parent, not their friend. Do children like boundaries and discipline? In the moment, no. But healthy discipline—just like healthy boundaries—creates stability and security throughout childhood and prepares children to flourish as adults. If you do not discipline your children they will resent you later for not doing your job as a parent.

"My child is already limited by a medical problem or tough life circumstances. How could I make his life harder?" Your child needs training for life just as much as any other child. His current challenge is already depriving him of the innocent childhood you wanted for him—don't also deprive him of the tools he needs to have a healthy relationship with the Lord and thrive as an adult. You might think you're easing his burden, but really you're doing him a disservice.

Personal Reflection

Write a statement below making a commitment to be consistent with discipline, even when it's uncomfortable for you as a mom.

So, what does healthy discipline look like on a practical level? I like to break it down into three C's: healthy discipline is compassionate, customized, and consistent.

Healthy discipline is **compassionate** because it's focused on the child's needs and experiences—not on releasing our emotion. Remember, teaching obedience is about preparing our children for healthy relationships with the Lord. It's in their best interest. In order to discipline compassionately, we must remove our own anger, disappointment, and other uncomfortable feelings from the situation.

Here's an amazing tip I learned from authors Foster Cline and Jim Fay in their book *Parenting with Love and Logic*: when your child disobeys a clear boundary, respond with a compassionate sound (such as an "aww")—and no other words. For example, let's say you told your child he could play with the spoon as long as he did not hit his sister or it would be taken away. Five minutes later, you watch your son whack his sister angrily with the spoon. Your instinct is probably to leap in with words: "Hey! I told you not to hit your sister. Now I'm going to have to take away the spoon." Don't. Instead, simply make a sigh that expresses empathy for your son, then take the spoon away with no further explanation.

There are a couple of keys to pulling this off. First, the tone of your "aww" is important. You are not expressing your disappointment in him. You're communicating that you, as his mother, feel for him. He made a bad choice and is about to experience the consequences for it. Second, you must refuse to argue about the situation. When you take the spoon from his hands and turn to walk away, he's going to react. He might cry, but it's more likely he'll argue. He'll say she pushed him or that he didn't hit her hard. You must keep your mouth shut. Do not engage—even if he seems confused—because any words at all interrupt his learning process. Give him a compassionate look that says, "I feel for you right now, but you brought this on yourself," and go about your business.

The first few times you do this, your child is likely to keep up his side of the argument, even following you from room to room pleading for a second chance. He might look confused, because this is a different response than what he's used to. But if you stand firm in your refusal to engage, he'll eventually learn that there's no room for argument when he disobeys. He'll learn that you mean business when you set a boundary, and that he can't talk his way out of experiencing the consequences of disobedience.

I've seen this simple practice make a huge difference in the lives of families. The main reason it's so effective is that it gives children space to really absorb the lesson that their choices lead to consequences. It also removes argument, making family life much more peaceful. Arguing with your children after they disobey is infuriating, and this is the moment when many moms lose their tempers. Saying "aww" and nothing else helps you keep your own emotions in check and prevents the situation from escalating. Your silence also forces your child to evaluate the situation on his own—something even toddlers are capable of doing. In all likelihood, he knew exactly why you took the spoon away. Even if he seemed confused, he's figuring it out. By not explaining or reiterating the boundary, you allow him to make the mental connection between his action and the consequence. With time, he'll get better at recognizing his choices and how his actions affect himself and others. He will begin to think about the consequences before he acts.

Note: It's totally OK—and even valuable—to have a conversation with your child about the situation later, after all the heightened emotions of the moment have dissipated. When you are tucking him into bed, ask him if he knows why you took away the spoon. If he genuinely doesn't know, remind him of the boundary you set and help him see that you were following through with the rule. Most likely, he knows. Talk with him about the choice he had and why it doesn't matter whether his sister did something to provoke him. He is only responsible for his actions. His sister is responsible for hers.

Personal Reflection

Describe a recent situation when you and your child argued over consequences. Do you feel like your child truly learned from that disciplinary experience?

Think of a disobedience scenario that's common in your home. Mentally prepare yourself in advance to say "aww" and nothing else. Write a reminder to yourself and place it somewhere you'll see it often.

Healthy discipline should be **customized**, just like the boundaries we set. Our goal is to use the least amount of pressure possible while still being effective. There are three factors to consider. First, of course, is the child's personality. For some children, a timeout is truly a serious consequence. For others, it might be a nice respite from chaos or space to conjure up retaliation. The kind of consequence you put in place should reflect the child's temperament.

The second factor is the boundary itself. As much as possible, we want to create natural consequences that make sense to kids. It makes sense that if you hit your sister with a spoon, the spoon will be taken away. When articulating boundaries to kids, use common sense to choose consequences that both fit the child's temperament and are relevant to the boundary.

The third factor is the severity of the disobedience. I like to break disobedience down into two major categories: weakness and willfulness. Weak disobedience is when children just can't help themselves. They get caught up in the moment and act on impulse without even thinking about the boundary or consequence at play. This is what's happening the vast majority of the time with most temperaments. In these situations, discipline helps them learn to step back, evaluate the consequences, and learn restraint. Discipline for this kind of disobedience should reflect natural consequences as much as possible, and therefore it varies widely.

Willful disobedience is another matter. It's when children know exactly what they're doing and do it anyway. They're not caught up in the moment. They haven't forgotten the rule. They are making a conscious choice to deliberately disobey or lie about something they've done. In these situations, there's a deeper heart issue at play, and discipline is about breaking a habit that could have devastating consequences later in life. Discipline for willful disobedience should be tough and standardized. For instance, you might implement a firm boundary that if any of your children choose to lie (in any situation), they will receive a spanking.

It's essential to treat willful disobedience differently because, in the long run, it has much more serious consequences for their life. You can think about the long-term difference by adding ten or twenty years to each kind of behavior. Consider an adult who didn't learn good self-awareness or restraint. This person is likely to have trouble controlling his impulses. He might say hateful things to his wife during arguments and spend too much money when he goes out with friends. He might have trouble resisting temptations, such as alcohol or pornography, and could fall into addiction. This is serious stuff, which is why we take all obedience seriously, but it's not as dangerous as the adult who intentionally breaks boundaries and uses deceit to get away with it. This adult is a danger to herself and others. She might destroy relationships by manipulating others or repeatedly cheating on her husband. She might embezzle company money, commit tax fraud, or engage in any number of unethical or illegal practices in order to get ahead—and, in doing so, she could seriously hurt other people.

Personal Reflection

Look back at the final reflection question in the previous chapter where you practiced writing some clear boundaries for your children. Take time now to finish that assignment by adding consequences to the statements that are relevant to your child's temperament and the boundary in question.

Now, let's talk for a minute about spanking. Spanking is taboo in our culture right now, and for good reason. Too many adults have physically abused their children and called it "spanking." But just because something can be abused doesn't mean it can't also be healthy. Physical discipline can be effective and loving. The key is to spank out of compassion, not anger.

Some of you might be wondering: "How on earth could hitting my child ever be compassionate?" Well, the same way all healthy boundaries and discipline are compassionate: they serve our children well in the long run by preparing them for healthy obedience to God. Yes, spanking is much more serious than taking away a spoon, but willful disobedience is much more serious than weak disobedience. Can timeouts, denying screen time, and other consequences be used instead? Absolutely. But for most children who exhibit willful disobedience, healthy spanking is much more effective.

Don and I used spanking for willful disobedience in our home, and I'll be honest with you: I hated it. It was never comfortable. But isn't that how it should be? We should never spank our children because it feels good to get our anger out. It should be something done separate from our own emotions, something done for their sake. There were times when I cried right along with my children, and those moments ended up being beautiful experiences of repentance, healing, and life change for my kids. For us, spanking was worth it because we believed it would help prevent our children from heading down destructive paths as adults. For assurance, we leaned on Proverbs 23:13–14: "Don't fail to discipline your children. The rod of punishment won't kill them. Physical discipline may well save them from death."

Here are the three steps to spanking in a healthy way:

1. **Wait a few minutes.** Never spank your child as a reaction. Give yourself time to calm down so you can spank for their sake—not out of anger. When your child disobeys in a way that calls for a spanking, respond with an initial "aww," then tell your child to wait for you in their bedroom. Say a rocket prayer and make sure you are calm. When it's time to spank, calmly ask your child to articulate the reason for the spanking. Make sure she is clear on why she's receiving a spanking before giving it.

2. **Give one to three swats with a flexible spatula.** The silicone will sting, but it won't damage her skin. Spank just hard enough to get a sad cry. If you get an angry or fake cry, you haven't spanked hard enough. Leave a couple of seconds between each swat, as this gives you an opportunity to gage her response and decide whether you need to swat a little harder the second or third time. It also insures you don't spank in anger.

3. **Give your child a hug and tell her how much you love her.** Hold her while she cries if she'll let you. Ask her how she feels. Most of the time, kids actually feel emotionally better

after a spanking because they instinctively know that once a penalty is paid, relationship is restored.

Personal Reflection

What are your initial thoughts and feelings on spanking?

Read Proverbs 19:18; 20:30; 22:15; and 29:17. Take a few minutes to pray. Ask God if spanking is a wise choice for your family. Write an overview of what these verses are saying.

Make a list of the kind of situations when spanking would be appropriate. What clear boundaries might you put in place to make your children aware of this change?

The final "C" for healthy discipline is to be **consistent**. Without consistency, discipline is scary and confusing for your kids, and all the security that comes with healthy boundaries and obedience is lost. Without consistency, your kids learn that obedience isn't about right and wrong—it's about Mom's mood. Your kids need to know what to expect from you. They need to understand that disobedience always has consequences. Plus, if you're inconsistent, they won't take your boundaries seriously, and you'll constantly fight an uphill battle.

Commit to the "aww" approach and use it every time. Make every effort to keep consequences consistent, regardless of the mood you're in. If you choose to employ spanking, try to do it the same way each time. The goal is for children to see boundaries and consequences as a consistent reality of life, not something that varies with Mom's whims.

Part of being consistent in your discipline is taking action immediately instead of giving your child second, third, and fourth chances to obey. For instance, let's say you ask your oldest daughter to take her little brother to the bathroom. She doesn't respond. Just in case she didn't hear you, you say it a little louder. She continues texting on her phone, so you say it again, even louder. Still no response. By the fourth time, your tone escalates and you are angry. "Chelsea!" you shout, "Take your brother to the bathroom now!" Finally, she responds—and probably looks at you like you're crazy for getting so upset.

We've all seen this kind of situation play out repeatedly. We think giving our children extra opportunities is compassionate. Here's the reality: in nearly every instance, your kid heard you the first time. At the very least, she heard your voice and chose not to ask what you said. Our kids know exactly how far they can push us. When we give second, third, and fourth chances like this, we set ourselves up for trouble. Not only do we put ourselves in a position to lose our temper, but we actually train our kids not to obey us until the fourth time. Therefore, the most compassionate choice is to discipline the first time, consistently. Remember that the point of all this is to teach our children healthy, submissive obedience that will transfer to God. Is fourth-time-around obedience the kind you want to transfer to the Most High?

If you've been in the habit of giving your kids multiple opportunities to obey before experiencing consequences, tell your kids that things are about to change by setting a new boundary: "I've noticed that you guys often make me repeat myself several times before you obey. Starting now, you will be disciplined if you do not respond right away when I ask you to do something." Do your best to avoid situations where your child genuinely might not hear you by speaking to them at close range instead of yelling from another room. If you must call from another room, start by simply calling your child's name in a positive tone. If you get a response, you know she can hear you.

Note: Sometimes, when it's time to follow through with consequences, you'll realize that the consequence you chose is too harsh for the infraction. In these cases, don't worry about being consistent with the boundary you set. Tell your child you are going to give a little grace and make the consequence lighter. In the event that you realize the consequence is too mild, stick to your word. It's not fair to issue consequences that are tougher than what you originally spelled out. Then, tell your child what the consequences will be in the future.

Personal Reflection

Describe a time when your child waited until the third or fourth time to obey. Describe his heart attitude. Was it rebellious or submissive when he finally obeyed? How did the delay create tension between you?

Personal Action

Have a family meeting. Apologize to your kids for the times you've lost your cool after they didn't obey you at first. Explain that you meant well by giving them second, third, and fourth chances, but you've learned that it's not actually good for anyone involved. Let them know that, from now on, you will only ask once. If they don't obey the first time, they'll be disciplined.

In closing, here's a quick mental checklist to run through whenever your child disobeys:

1. **Check your heart.** Are you emotional or angry? If so, send up a rocket prayer asking for love and compassion and take a breath before you speak.
2. **Ask yourself if you set clear boundaries for this situation.** If so, then move on to the next step. But if you haven't, take time now to clearly state a boundary for the future. Remember, it's not fair to discipline your children for something you haven't said is wrong. Boundaries always need to come first.
3. **Follow through with discipline.** If you said you'd take the spoon away, take the spoon away—*the first time*. Don't let yourself get sucked into an argument.

Dealing with disobedience is annoying and time consuming. Nobody enjoys battling a toddler who doesn't want to put on his shoes when you are late for an appointment. It's often easier to let the misbehavior slide. But never forget that teaching true obedience is not about our convenience. It's about preparing our children for a healthy relationship with God.

With that goal in mind, we must take obedience seriously and do what it takes to teach it well. We must set clear boundaries and respond to disobedience with discipline that is compassionate, customized, and consistent. Even if it feels uncomfortable in the moment, we are giving our children a great gift. In fact, God says in Deuteronomy that we are commanded to honor our fathers and mothers "so that you may live long and that it may go well with you." Obedience is good for the obedient.

Rocket Prayer

"Lord, help me to compassionately teach this child to obey."

Say this prayer when you are irritated by your child's behavior. Say this prayer when you're tempted to ignore your child's behavior. With these simple words, we remind ourselves of our goal and call on God to help us achieve it.

Prayer of Response

Before you close this workbook for the rest of the week, take a few minutes to write a prayer of response to God. First, thank him for ways he has been good to you. Then, tell him what you're thinking and feeling as you process what you've learned.

FINISHING WELL

1 WEEK

In this concluding chapter, we reflect on our growth and make a practical plan for parenting with purpose in the years to come.

18

cultivating character

[Wisdom] will guide you down delightful paths;
all her ways are satisfying.

PROVERBS 3:17

This is the end. You made it. This workbook has been incredibly challenging, and I hope you feel proud of the ways you've grown. You have deepened your self-awareness and exercised your self-control. You've torn down walls and false hopes and fake idols and, in their wake, you've build a strong foundation in the Lord. You've built something to stand on. And, in doing so, you've become a much better mom for your kids.

Personal Reflection

Take twenty minutes to go back through each chapter in the workbook. Using a journal or separate piece of paper, write down at least one thing from each chapter that stood out to you.

Next, spend a few minutes journaling about how this journey has changed your heart, your life, and your parenting.

This is also not the end. By the last page of this chapter you will be done with this workbook, yes, but you will not be done working on that foundation. If your relationship with the Lord is to remain strong enough to stand on, you must nurture it. Relationships are never finished. They are always changing. They grow deeper and they fall apart. Know that the Lord is always—always, always, always—fully committed to you. His hand is always extended in invitation to you. Because you know what? He simply cannot get enough of you.

Personal Reflection

Are there any areas of growth you need to recommit to? For instance, did you practice thankfulness for three weeks, then get out of the habit? Since working on forgiveness, have you fallen back into holding grudges? Name the top two to three things covered in this workbook that you need to work on and make a fresh commitment.

Daily life with your children may seem mundane, but the Lord has invited you on a grand journey. He is up to something—in your life, in your family, and in your city—and he's invited you to participate. The seasons of my life that I've been the most connected to the Lord have been the richest and the most exciting. I've seen the little miracles that I otherwise wouldn't have noticed, and I've felt part of God's great plan to redeem his creation.

At the most personal level, you are invited on a journey to become the person God created you to be. This workbook has been a start, a foundation. But a foundation is not a house. Houses come in all shapes and styles. Every one of us, regardless of our unique personality, was designed to thrive when we are thankful, forgiving, obedient, generous—all the qualities we worked on in these pages. But God also created each one of us with a unique purpose, and your job now is to continue deepening your connection to the Lord, learning from him, and discovering the unique plan he has for your life. You have something to stand on now. So stand, and start building your house.

Personal Action

Read Romans 12. Say a prayer of thanks to God for all he's taught you, and ask him to help you continue becoming the person he created you to be. Write down anything you hear from him.

Your job is also to help your children become the people God created them to be. Because, after all, part of your purpose is to nanny these particular children of the King. To this end, we have one final project: craft a Character Plan for each of your children.

We know our big-picture goal is to raise godly kids ready for service to the King. Each of you wrote your own version of that goal in the first chapter. But what does that mean for your children as individuals? How can you customize your parenting to help each child become who God created him to be? A Character Plan is a simple way to work toward this, and it essentially revolves around two questions: Who does God want this child to be when she reaches adulthood, and how can I help her get there?

Crafting a Character Plan begins with casting a vision for core family values. These are godly character qualities that you hope every one of your children will embody, regardless of their unique personality. These might be qualities like prioritizing God above all else, loving your neighbor as yourself, living an honest life, being engaged in community, valuing the dignity of all people, and practicing thankfulness. They're qualities that help your children draw closer to God and be more like Christ—qualities that help your children learn to stand on God alone.

Note that none of these examples have anything to do with hobbies or interests. We're not talking about whether our children will be creative, athletic, or adventurous. We're talking about their hearts.

Now, here's the risk associated with establishing a Character Plan: if you aren't careful, you might push your child toward your own ideal of what a person should be—not toward the person God has created her to be. For instance, based on your own values and personality, your list of qualities might cast a vision for a child who grows up to be gentle, nonconfrontational, and encouraging to those around him. Maybe that's who you are, and that's a wonderful person to have in the Kingdom. But what if God created your son to be a passionate activist on behalf of the poor? His natural strengths might not be on your personal list of core family values. In fact, his natural strengths might even feel uncomfortable to you.

So, how do we mitigate this risk? The most important thing is to invite God into the process. We must ask him what character qualities *he* wants us to instill in our children, and we must remain open-minded about who he has created our children to be. After all, they're his children first and foremost. We'll also be intentional about inviting our spouses and children into the conversation so we're not making decisions solo.

Personal Reflection

Take a minute to pray. Ask the Lord what character qualities he wants you to instill in your family.

Make a list of the top five or six qualities you'd like to see in all of your children. You can use phrases or individual words—whatever is easiest for you. If you find it hard to come up with qualities, try thinking about people you admire. Still stuck? Try simply Googling "character qualities" for a comprehensive list. Sometimes looking at a list can help you think about which qualities matter most to you and your family.

Personal Action

Have a family meeting. Share your list, and ask what qualities they'd like to add or subtract. It's important to have your whole family's buy-in.

When your list is final, come up with a creative way to document these core values in your home so everyone is reminded daily. For instance, a friend of mine made a poster and put it on her dining room wall. Find something that works for you, and get it done. It's so beneficial for all of you to be reminded of these values on a regular basis. Write your plan here.

The second big piece of a Character Plan is exploring how to actually cultivate these core family values in your children—especially considering that your children are unique individuals with their own sets of strengths and weaknesses.

In my home, honesty was one of our core family values, and teaching it to my children meant taking a very individualized approach. Cammy seemed to come out of the womb honest. She was so honest she'd remind me to spank her when she'd disobeyed! I encouraged and rewarded her honesty, and that was enough. But Blair—well, Blair was another story. He was quick to lie in order to get his way. With Blair, I had to establish a couple of extra boundaries around honesty, and I had to question what he told me in a way I never did with Cammy. Teaching Blair to be honest took a lot of attention and intentionality. But you know what? Blair turned into an incredible person with great depth of character. He also had other natural gifts that my daughter had to work hard to learn.

The next set of questions will help you think intentionally about teaching your core family values to each of your unique children. For the sake of sanity, I recommend focusing on just a couple of qualities at a time. Start by choosing one quality to focus on family-wide for six months to a year at a time. Then, choose one additional value to focus on with each child during that time frame—whichever quality seems to be their greatest weakness at the time. For instance, you might focus on peacemaking family-wide, then also work on honesty with your daughter and generosity with your son.

If your children are too young to really exhibit any strengths or weaknesses in these areas, simply spend the next few minutes brainstorming ways to begin encouraging two of your family values. For instance, if perseverance is on your list, you might come up with little games to help your toddler practice overcoming obstacles. Or, you might simply be mindful to step back a little and allow your baby to try things on his own instead of always intervening to help.

Personal Reflection

Choose one core family value to focus on family-wide over the next six months to a year.

Name a few practical ways you can encourage and cultivate that quality in each of your children.

Name a few practical ways you can work on that quality in yourself.

Identify which core family value is the greatest weakness for each of your children.

Name a few ways you can proactively work on each child's weakness over the next six months to a year.

The final piece of a Character Plan focuses less on what we want for our children and more on who they are already—just one more step to help insure we don't impose our own ideals onto our children and, instead, remain open to God's vision for them.

Our task is to simply look at our children's personalities. Is your son fearless? Analytical? Bossy? Go-with-the-flow? Even if your child is only a year old, the odds are good you can name at least one or two key characteristics. It's OK if the characteristics that come to mind seem negative, such as stubbornness. Our children are blessed with many gifts, but when they're young those gifts often show up in a negative way. They simply haven't learned to use them in a positive way yet.

The reality is that almost every trait can either become a force for good in your child's life or a serious problem. For example, let's say your daughter is particularly stubborn. You've undoubtedly already seen how that trait can be problematic, and it's easy to imagine how it could cause trouble in the long run. But there can also be a good side to stubbornness. Usually, we call it by a different name: "tenacity," "determination," or perhaps "conviction." Maybe your daughter has what it takes to do what's right in the face of peer pressure. Maybe she's the type who will never give up, even when the obstacles are overwhelming. If nurtured in the right way, that stubbornness could turn into a wonderful gift.

Nurturing your child's characteristics in positive ways starts with simply reframing them in your mind. If you can think about your daughter's stubbornness as untrained tenacity, you're more likely to respond to her and guide her in a helpful way.

Personal Reflection

First, take a minute to pray that God will help you see your children the way he does. Ask him to help you imagine who he created them to be. Then, focusing on one child at a time, work through the following:

Name two or three key characteristics that define your child's personality at this point in his life. Try to choose positive words, such as "tenacious" instead of "stubborn" or "sensitive" instead of "dramatic." Remember, you might just be seeing the negative side of a trait because your child hasn't learned to use it well yet.

If those characteristics develop in a positive way, what could they look like in your child when he's a teen or adult? How might God use them?

Name a few practical ways you can encourage those characteristics in a positive direction over the next six months to a year.

Now you have the makings of a Character Plan. You've chosen family-wide values and considered how to cultivate them in each child. You've explored the unique gifting God has given your children. All that's left is to put it all together.

Personal Action

Take several minutes to put all this together in a place you can revisit again and again. I recommend creating separate documents on a computer for each child. On each, list your core family values at the top. Then, name the two values you're focusing on now (one that's family-wide, one that's specific to this child's weakness) and your ideas for teaching those values. Finally, add this child's key characteristics and your ideas for nurturing those traits in a healthy direction.

Create a separate character plan for yourself, as well. At the top, list your core family values. Then, name the value your family is focusing on now, and write your ideas for growing in that area yourself. Finally, list the areas of growth you recommitted to earlier in this chapter.

Set reminders on your phone or calendar to revisit these documents every six months or every year. You can choose what frequency is right for you.

When you revisit your Character Plans over the years, update your core family values as needed. Also, reaffirm the need to continue working on one of last year's character qualities or pick new qualities to focus on. Check in on your own progress, and set fresh goals for the next six months to a year as needed.

When you revisit your Character Plan, also make adjustments to the portion about your child's key characteristics. Children change a lot over the course of a year. Are those still your child's dominant characteristics? If not, work through the exercise again. Don't worry about the inconsistency of this. As your children age, their truly dominant characteristics will become clearer and clearer. What matters, even when they're very young, is that you are paying attention to who they are and encouraging them to be the best version of that. This will help you remain open to whoever God created them to be.

In my own experience, having a Character Plan for each child was foundational to parenting with purpose. It gave me something to lean on, to turn back to when I felt like parenting was a constant game of catch-up. It helped me stay focused on long-term goals and approach boundaries and discipline with intentionality. I hope that it will do the same for you.

It has been an honor to walk alongside you these last few months. Even though I'll never read your responses and will likely not hear your stories, I feel you've let me into your life and your heart. I want you to know it is a privilege. I hope my own stories and experiences have blessed you as you built a stronger foundation in the Lord. Instead of concluding this chapter with a rocket prayer to use, I want to finish by sharing my prayer for each one of you.

Lord, thank you for this mom. Thank you for calling her to be a nanny to your beloved children. May she truly know just how much you love her. May she remember that every one of your commandments is a gift for her benefit—that you designed and created her, and you know exactly what her heart needs. Bless this mom as she raises your children for service in the Kingdom. Give her wisdom, and empower her with the fruits of your Spirit. Thank you, Lord, for giving her a foundation to stand on. Amen.

Finally, be reminded of this promise from your King, found in Jeremiah 29:11–13: "'I know the plans I have for you,' says the Lord. 'They are plans for good and not for disaster, to give you a future and a hope. In those days when you pray, I will listen. If you look for me wholeheartedly, you will find me.'"

Personal Journal

Personal Journal

Personal Journal

Personal Journal

Acknowledgments

My husband, Don, supported and encouraged me through every step of this project. On the days I would have preferred cleaning toilets to writing, he reminded me of the ultimate goal.

My oldest, Danae, broke me into motherhood easy. Her gentleness and sensitivity taught me to love others unconditionally.

My oldest son, Blair, helped me grow the most as a parent. His gentle sweetness and challenging spirit taught me patience and kindness.

My youngest daughter, Cammy, inspired me to look for the best in others with her honesty, openness, and zest for life. She taught me to enjoy people for who they are.

My youngest, Cavan, taught me to show gentleness and sensitivity to others with his loving care and protectiveness.

My co-writer, Melissa, listened to me talk, read my manuscript, and turned my ideas into this beautiful workbook.

There are so many other women in my life who have encouraged and shaped me. Special thanks to Cammy Cavan, Teri Sharp, Cheryl Kent, Mel Kent, and Kristi Hayworth.

About the Authors

Brenda Jacobson is a mother to four grown children and has been mentoring moms in churches for over fifteen years, and women recovering from addiction or reentering society after stints in prison. Her passion for helping women has taken her around the world, from a prostitution recovery center in Nicaragua to the top of Mt. Kilimanjaro. She lives in Portland, Oregon, with her husband of forty years, Don.

Melissa Binder is a writer and editor who specializes in putting words to the ideas in other people's heads. In a former life, she was an award-winning journalist. She lives in a bright blue house in Portland, Oregon, with her husband and young son.

ZEALbooks

Portland, Oregon

Zeal Books is a new publisher dedicated to world-changing ideas. We're focused and founded on love—love for our authors and love for their books. And love makes you zealous. Zeal's commitment to its authors, readers, and accounts is to only publish books we're zealous for—books the world needs.

Visit us online for news, resources, and more, at zealbooks.com, or find us on social media:

 @ZealBks

 @ZealBks

 facebook.com/zealbks